REMOTE PERCEPTIONS

REMOTE PERCEPTIONS

Out-of-Body Experiences,
Remote Viewing,
and Other Normal Abilities

Angela
Thompson Smith

HAMPTON ROADS
PUBLISHING COMPANY, INC.

for the evolving human spirit

Cover design by Marjoram Productions
Cover painting by Nick Gonzalez

For information write:

Hampton Roads Publishing Company, Inc.
134 Burgess Lane
Charlottesville, VA 22902

Or call: 804-296-2772
FAX: 804-296-5096
e-mail: hrpc@hrpub.com
Web site: http://www.hrpub.com

If you are unable to order this book from your local
bookseller, you may order directly from the publisher.
Quantity discounts for organizations are available.
Call 1-800-766-8009, toll-free.

Library of Congress Catalog Card Number: 98-71585

ISBN 1-57174-109-7

10 9 8 7 6 5 4 3 2 1

Printed on acid-free recycled paper in Canada

Dedicated to

Hal Puthoff

One of the first pioneers in
remote viewing and inspiration to
my journey of exploration

TABLE OF CONTENTS

Prologue to the Phenomenon • Substantiating the Illusory • The Origin of the Journey • The Phoenix Awakes • The Teacher Appears • Genetics or Environment? • Nocturnal Visions • Exceptional Human Experiences • Precognitive Puzzles • Recreating the Cosmos • Marital Misfortunes • Meditations in the Midlands • Metaphysical Manifestations • Researching the Literature • Astral Travels and Astral Doings • Pragmatic Applications • The Psychophysical Institute, Oxford • Almost Full Circle • Letting Go of the Past

Inner Outer Space • Jupiter Probes • Space Junk • Zero Rads • Perceiving Glitches • Consulting for Psi Tech • The Rings of Saturn • Unusual Personal Events • The Demise of the Mars Observer • CSETI and Coherent Thought Sequencing • Meeting of the Minds • A Different Kind of Contact • A Jigsaw of Events • Data Downloads of a Mysterious Kind • Unidentified Flying Objects • The Appearance of the Rub Tub • Solid Illusions • Confronting the Monitor • Communicating with the Cosmos • Mysterious Area 51 • Where's the Roswell Wreckage? • Solitary Isolation • The Four Corners Incident • Remote Viewing or remote viewing? • Remote Applications

Instant Karmic Replays • Recovery through Reliving • This Mortal Coil • Spiritual Explorations • Of Ghosts and Goblins • Coping with Negative or Unwanted Intrusions • The Christos Experience • Iron Age Avon • Searching for Confirmation • Time Transportation • Viewing Your Own Grandmother • Burned as a Witch • The King's Mistress • Following the Trail of the Herb Strewer • The Rich, Bored Widow of Shropshire • The Short, Sad Life of Nicola Dubrec • The Naughty Italian Nun

Chapter Four: Looking Forward . . . . . .

Fixing the Ozone Hole • The 2030 Exodus • The Big One in the Big Apple • Future Earth Changes

Chapter Five: Participation . . . .

The Psychophysical Research Laboratories (PRL) • The Mind-Science Foundation • Princeton Engineering Anomalies Research (PEAR) Laboratory • The National ESP Laboratory • Precognitive Remote Perception (PRP) • The Unabomber Case • Children and Remote Viewing • Developing Your Remote Perception Skills • Practical Advice to the Beginner • Extended Remote Viewing or ERV • Remote Perception Applications • Practical Considerations • Beginner's Luck • Questions and Answers • The Harmony of Opposites Method • Remote Tracking • Coordinate Remote Viewing • The Ritual Method • Technical Aids • The Monroe Method • Meditation Method • The Christos Technique • The Imagery Method • Ophiel's "Little System" • Associative Remote Viewing (ARV) • Future Memory Technique • Controlled Remote Viewing • Review of Methods • Educational Courses in Parapsychology • Becoming Involved in Psi Research

SECTION TWO

Appendix A: Altered States of Consciousness .

A Rose by Any Other Name • Business Applications • A Rebirth of Human Consciousness • Facilitating Altered States of Consciousness • Cultural Considerations • To Sleep: To Dream

Appendix B: History . . . .

Historical Considerations • Theosophical Teachings on Astral Travel • David-Neal Manifests a Tulpa • The Blue Nun of Agreda • The Bilocation Case of Alphonsus Liguori • The Notorious Count St. Germain • Consciousness-Matter Interactions • Waking Dreams • Charles Tart Studies Robert Monroe and Miss Z • The Demographics of OBEs • The ASPR and Alex Tanous • The ASPR and Ingo Swann • Stanford Research Institute (SRI) • Stuart Harary and the Psychical Research Foundation • Jack Houck and the Magical 7.8 Hz • Positive Side Effects of Remote Perception

FOREWORD

The importance of Angela Thompson Smith and this book might better be grasped if you draw a large circle on a piece of paper. Call the outer side of the circle "the present." Put a dot in the middle of the circle. Call it "earliest antiquity."

Fill in the circle with millions and millions of dots. Each of these dots represents some one individual who, from antiquity to the present, has experienced the consciousness states Angela describes and discusses herein.

Now, just on the other side of the circle, in the "present," make a lot of little squiggles, hundreds and thousands of them, until not one more squiggle fits around the circle's entire circumference. These squiggles represent those in "the present" who experience approximately what the dots from "earliest antiquity" have. Perhaps you are one of them.

Angela Thompson Smith, delightful and energetic and ardent, like the rest of all "experiencers" is one of those squiggles in "the present." But she has written *this book*, which surveys the nature of what all the other millions of dots have experienced or what the squiggles experience today.

This book, I think, is a welcome, even necessary, blending of personal experiencing and data—both historical data and what might be called "clinical" or "research" facts. It's usually said that experiencers who can write lucidly of their experiencing, as Angela does, are "articulate." But when researchers, such as Angela *also* is, write about clinical facts or research data, whether they are articulate or not is often overlooked. Angela is articulate herein, whether regarding her autobiographical or research experience.

Thus, Angela and her book are among the unique; for, as I've found in my own twenty-two years of laboratory research, it's more usual for experiencers to be researched (and "tested") by non-experiencers who hardly ever research (or even wonder about) why they themselves are non-experiencers. Yet Angela possesses a highly qualified background as a researcher, and is personally articulate as well. She is also one more thing; she is what is called "objective" throughout, objectivity being considered exceedingly important in research, even by some researchers who are not quite so themselves.

One of the problems of Angela's "field" of study is that it is a very big one. For you see, when all is said and done, that field is *consciousness*—its vistas, its potentials and possibilities. It is even bigger when you consider that all human beings possess consciousness in some form or format, and so her "field" is as big as the human species itself. So, the problem is that if you take an interest in consciousness, you soon can't keep it a small thing, you can't divide it up into tiny categories and honestly conclude very much. Whatever *consciousness* may be, it's *not* a small thing.

Rather, it's not a small thing from the moment you decide to go outside your local "universe" and have a look at the larger consciousness "universe" all around. Beginning with autobiographical materials, Angela develops her book into an invitational trek into and through this larger consciousness universe.

Angela has elected to present, as foci, what is presently being called "out-of-body experience" (OBE) and "remote viewing." Even after two decades of researching them myself, I'm not sure they are appropriate terms. In any event, as Angela established what these terms mean today, they have in the past been referred to under other terms, most equally valid, if they are understood.

But even if we might get snarled into somewhat stereotyped terminology, still her points are made increasingly clear: human consciousness is *not* trapped within the bio-body, or within one's local consciousness universe, or within socially-engineered consciousness formats. And this, I think, is her wonderful book's basic message; a message carefully and arduously constructed and supported by numerous scientific references.

The book goes, though, somewhat *beyond* scientific references, which is natural enough, because if there is one thing all our still evolving science have not yet comprehended very well, it is *consciousness*. In this sense, the usual mandate of scientists (and many parapsychologists) to stay *within* what is scientifically known is not very valid—not only because we can't learn *more* by obeying the mandate, but because the mandate itself will eventually change its contours and incorporate much of what had been rejected before. Change, yes, but only because of some "squiggle" like Angela Thompson Smith—an experiencer both exceedingly articulate and scientifically based, and an explorer and frontier fighter person as well.

Ingo Swann
New York

ACKNOWLEDGMENTS

Thanks are due to the many people who have encouraged me and assisted in the writing of this book: first, my dear friend and companion David A Smith for his patience and support; Barbara Flick for her never-ceasing encouragement; Marita Lindlau for her grounding influence; Paula Underwood who taught me to present my writing in three different ways: once for the right ear, once for the left ear, and once for the heart; and, to Marjorie Paines, my aunt, who always told me to "write about what you know." Many thanks also to Ryan Wood for help in locating references and individuals, and to Ryan and Ron Blackburn for allowing me to use many of the projects that were undertaken for Intuition Services; Gary Trujillo for references and information on astral travel; Stanley Krippner of Saybrook Institute for very important comments on definitions and format; Holmes (Skip) Atwater of the Monroe Institute for important input regarding Robert Monroe, Pat Price, and the Monroe Institute and also for introducing me to Hampton Roads Publishing Company; Paul Smith, and Joe McMoneagle for insights into definitions of remote viewing; William Jack for editorial comments; Dean Radin for his helpful and encouraging comments; and many other friends and colleagues for their encouragement and support.

PREFACE

Right here, at the beginning, I would like to tell you something about who I am and why this book was written. Although much of this book may seem academic, I have tried to introduce the personal touch—to remind the reader that I am a real person with real emotions. I, too, have experienced all the fears, worries, and anxieties that can arise when you are trying to understand a new phenomenon. I, too, have felt alone with my experiences. I have wondered if I was "normal," and I had anxieties about the reactions of my family, friends, and colleagues. On the other hand, there has been a wonderful sense of curiosity and excitement in my journey to investigate the phenomenon and its practical applications.

In October of 1978 I became aware that I had an ability that was not shared by many people. Until then I thought that my out-of-body experiences, or OBEs, were a common occurrence, like dreaming, that everybody regularly experienced. The phenomenon has been widely recorded in both parapsychological and orthodox medical journals. During an OBE the individual has a vivid feeling of being some distance away from his physical body, which may be seen lying inert below the person experiencing the event. Some people see a connecting silver cord. Often a crisis between life and death initiates the experience, and it has also been seen as a psychic experience which some people can achieve at will. Now, in the 20th century, the subject of mental travel and its practical application is coming under scientific scrutiny. The mysticism is falling away to reveal a phenomenon of great scientific and social interest. During many years of academic pursuit I have gained a graduate degree in psychology, as well as training as a nurse and social worker. To supplement this education I sought out professional research institutions and organizations doing research in more esoteric topics. During the 1980s, I was fortunate to be involved in many research programs where I was able to explore paranormal phenomena. These investigations took me to such places as Oxford in England, Princeton University in New Jersey, and, through remote participation, to research institutions in Texas, Virginia, and California.

In 1991 I was invited to participate as a consultant for Psi Tech and, a few years later, for Intuition Services. The goal of both groups was to base remote viewing (RV) on a professional and business foundation and work for its recognition as a marketable skill. Remote viewing, in its simplest definition, is the name given to a formal, trained skill where professionals are able to describe geographic locations, events, and people at a distance from the viewer—even halfway around the world.

I have finally answered my own question. I have discovered that the phenomenon is real, that it has always been available to us but unrecognized, and that it has far-reaching practical applications for humanity.

Remote Perceptions was conceived out of the need for an updated accounting of American and international parapsychological (psi) research, specifically involving remote viewing, and the practical application of this ability. The last ten years has seen a decline in parapsychological research facilities but there has also been a redefinition taking place. Researchers in the conventional sciences, particularly in the fields of physics, statistics, and medicine, have become very interested in psi and the next decade promises great advances in psi research. In particular, there have been efforts to put psi into practical application with the formation of groups who are undertaking technical remote viewing, in applying mind-body concepts in the field of medicine, and in the discovery that human consciousness plays a vital role in our understanding of reality. I consider myself a pioneer and a heretic. Despite dire warnings from scientific colleagues and friends, including parapsychologists, I have dared to wander onto unexplored paths.

During the course of writing I have tried to remember some advice given to me by my Native American friend, educator and writer, Paula Underwood. She advised that whatever one says or writes should be explained from three perspectives: once for the left ear, once for the right ear, and once for the heart. You will find that this book is not just a scientific textbook (speaking to the right ear), neither is it a collection of anecdotal material (speaking to the left ear). It includes both, and speaks, honestly, from the heart.

One of the major questions asked, of the remote viewing (RV) phenomenon, has been whether some aspect of human consciousness actually leaves the body during remote viewing (as in an out-of-body experience) or whether we are processing information within some internally-generated, imaginal world? Are out-of-body experiences and remote viewing the same or different? Or are they different aspects of the same phenomenon?

According to critic and parapsychologist Susan Blackmore, "An OBE is an experience in which a person seems to perceive the world from a location outside his physical body. In this state they can see and hear events and conversations that cannot be perceived from his actual physical location." Ingo Swann, artist, writer, researcher, originator of the term "remote viewing" or RV, initially described RV as "a mixture of what used to be called clairvoyance, thought transference, and telepathy. It is a process where a viewer perceives information about a distant location using something other than the known five senses."

According to some of the more orthodox remote viewers, who were trained by Swann for the military unit at Fort Meade, the term remote viewing can only be used to refer to the very disciplined research and application RV protocol of controlled remote viewing or CRV. However, throughout this book, the term remote viewing will be based on the usage given to it by Ingo Swann and the original research team at Stanford Research Institute in California. According to Puthoff and Targ in their classic 1976 paper entitled "A Perceptual Channel for Information Transfer over Kilometer Distances":

> As observed in the laboratory, the basic phenomenon appears to cover a range of subjective experiences variously referred to in the literature as autoscopy (in the medical literature); exteriorization or dissociation (psychological literature); simple clairvoyance; traveling clairvoyance, or out-of-body experience (parapsychological literature); or astral projection (occult literature). We choose the term "remote viewing" as a neutral descriptive term, free from prior associations and bias as to mechanism.

Since the early research at the American Society for Psychical Research (ASPR) and, later, at the Stanford Research Institute (SRI), the term "remote viewing" has come into *general* usage, usually to denote the ability to perceive hidden or remote information by anomalous or psychic means.

Swann has written that he has always been aware that his spirit was not confined to his physical body. He suggests that mental travel is merely an extension through time and space of individual consciousness. He also believes that the ability to have such experiences is not a special talent but a natural function of human consciousness. However, remote viewing, as a *protocol*, is different from a simple OBE. Swann has added his concern that the RV term is often misused. It was originally coined to identify a specific kind of experiment, rather than a particular kind of psi ability. According to Swann, the remote viewing model consists of five definite components: a subject; active ESP abilities; a distant target; the subject's recorded responses; and confirmatory positive feedback. When one of these component parts is missing, remote viewing has not taken place. During an OBE, the first three of these components might be present, but recording of the experience and confirmatory feedback are not always present.

Leonard Buchanan, one of the original members of the military remote viewing team during the 1980s, adds his own concerns. Buchanan was trained in Swann's protocol, which Swann called controlled remote viewing (CRV). CRV was designed, for the military, as a very structured, disciplined protocol, employing strict controls, and was to be carried out using a human monitor. Buchanan has modified the CRV nomenclature, at the request of Swann, but still adheres to Swann's original concept of a highly structured process. Buchanan believes that CRV and OBEs are completely different things. He feels that the term, "remote viewing," is used by a lot of people to mean different things. Remote viewing, he says, originally meant the set of protocols which, under strict, scientific controls, could be used to test, evaluate, quantify, and prove innate psychic ability. Once it gained scientific respect, almost everyone who had done anything "psychic" jumped on the bandwagon and started calling what they did "remote viewing." Therefore, he adds, a distinction has had to be made between the New Age adoption of "remote viewer" to mean anything and everything psychic, and "controlled remote viewing" as a definite protocol, with certain rules and regulations.

Buchanan goes on to describe what CRV is and how it might differ from an OBE. In CRV, he states, you begin by getting your conscious mind to accept information from your subconscious mind, mainly by using the body (your writing hand) as a sort of "translator" between the two. Very quickly, you begin to get impressions which are also body-centered: smells, tastes, textures, temperatures, visuals of color, brightness, etc. As you continue, these "sensories" become more and more vivid and realistic as you stop paying attention to the world around you and start paying more and more attention to the impressions coming from your subconscious.

He reminds students that these sensations are coming primarily through the "physical mind" or autonomic nervous system. As the conscious mind "buys into" these impressions, and especially because you are involving the body in the process, they begin to take over your awareness. At some point you have what is called "Perfect Site Integration or PSI." Ingo Swann termed this "bilocation." That is, says Buchanan, you buy into the impressions coming from your subconscious mind so solidly that you totally ignore the world around you and begin to see the site, feel the wind on your face, smell the air, etc. In effect, he adds, your conscious/subconscious/body combination has formed for you a sort of self-contained, virtual reality—you have bought into it completely.

Buchanan continues by saying that the PSI condition is one which transfixes the viewer who experiences the site just exactly as though he were there. That means that, in order to get a report of it, you have to wait until they "get back." Then all you get is a summary. The trick in CRV is to take the viewer as close to the PSI condition as possible, without letting him get sucked all the way into it. He reminds students that although PSI happens rarely, once they "buy into it" totally, the information collection goes on hold. Buchanan concludes that as much as people want to make CRV (or any other form of remote viewing) and OBE the same thing, the fact is that they just are not.

Historically and culturally, OBEs and distant viewing appeared to have been complementary human faculties. However, in modern times, scientific methods have been used to study various aspects of this ability and the two phenomena of OBEs and remote perception/remote viewing have come to be seen as two distinct entities with a great deal of grey area in between.

As an individual who has experienced OBEs since childhood, and conducted remote viewing (both in the research laboratory and in practice), I feel qualified to comment on the topic under discussion. I think that OBEs and remote viewing exist on a continuum of experience, beginning, perhaps, with simple OBEs (where the viewer lifts out and floats suspended over his inert body), along a line to remote perception (where the viewer perceives geographic locations separated from the viewer by time and distance), and to a point where the individual is able to access information from these remote locations. Somewhere along this continuum lies the ability to actively interact with, and perhaps even affect, events, people, and things at these distant locations.

Over past 20 years, experimental protocols have changed as different laboratories have studied remote perception. New terminology, such as precognitive remote perception and anomalous information transfer, as well as remote viewing, has been introduced. The world has claimed the term remote viewing as its own, and it now appears to have two definitions: remote viewing as experimental protocol, and remote viewing as a generalized human ability. Perhaps, we need to generate yet another name for remote viewing. After all, each culture and historic time has had a definite name for the ability; why not one for the 21st century? I would suggest Human Remote Sensing as a general definition.

It has only been in the past two decades that controlled experimental protocols have been designed specifically to explore remote perception. Several commercial groups have been applying remote viewing on a practical basis, offering to remote view for business, industry and government. Their efforts have shown a significant degree of success. According to these groups remote viewing is a learnable skill.

I believe that human consciousness is not tied irrevocably to the body but that it is a mobile function of the human system and, under certain circumstances, consciousness and the body can separate. Under these conditions, perceptions can be experienced with a faculty separate from our regular five senses.

A point made by Lyn Buchanan, in my estimation, sums up the dilemma regarding definitions of remote viewing. He advises the student to look at what he writes about controlled remote viewing and Perfect Site Integration and says, "See if that fits your definition of OBE. If so, then they are the same. If they are not, then they are different." The debate continues . . . . But, I will repeat here that the original definition of remote viewing, documented by Puthoff and Targ in 1976, will be used throughout this book.

Remote viewing and OBEs, despite all the current confusions over terminology, are normal, human abilities, and we have always possessed these faculties. I believe that they are as much a part of our normal experience as memory, learning, and language, and deserve to be studied in the same manner as these other human abilities. Also, like musical or math ability, some people have more of a natural talent, others need training. I did not always know this.

My life has taken many interesting turns. In 1992, I moved to Las Vegas to help establish the Bigelow Foundation, a philanthropic organization. The Foundation focused on topics that have not yet been accepted into the scientific mainstream, such as psi, UFO research, survival issues, and alternative medicine. The Bigelow Foundation ran surveys, organized conferences, conducted research projects, and helped some of the major researchers in the psi and UFO fields continue their work.

Now, I am working for myself. I have formed a non-profit organization called the Inner Vision Institute, to teach extended remote viewing (ERV). Currently located in Las Vegas, the Institute has hosted students from around the world, as well as the United States. Inner Vision teaches many of the remote viewing techniques—which have established track records in the research community—under the title of extended remote viewing. One of our goals is to develop a retreat site where many aspects of remote perception can be learned.

I have been asked if my experiences are a form of OBE, or is it that, in our fullest, truest state, we are not in the body unless that body is the entire created universe? This is a tough question. I believe that the answer is: both views are correct. It is all a matter of labeling. When I was discovering my abilities in my twenties, the term OBE was the one generally used to describe what I do. I now consider myself a remote viewer, as well as someone who has OBEs.

We are made of the *stuff* of the universe, so, in that sense, we are part of the universe. However, we are totally unique beings. My consciousness is who I am, whether I am in the monist state (mind and body cooperating as a total unit) or in a dualist mode (mind and body able to separate and exist independently). Perhaps we can travel within the universe, and understand it, because we are part of it.

Like my childhood heroines, Elizabeth Fry, an 18th century Quaker and social worker who went alone into England's notorious slum prisons, and Florence Nightingale, who nursed the sick at Scutari during the Crimean War, I consider myself a pioneer. I have dared to wander onto unexplored paths: angels tread where wise men fear to go. These paths have included interfacing with other-dimensional entities, experiencing OBEs, precognition, psychokinesis, remote viewing, and trying to understand all of these human experiences as a whole.

My views regarding my abilities and experiences have come full circle. When I was a child, I thought that everybody had the same abilities I had and experienced the same things that I did. I did not think of myself as having exceptional human experiences. Working with established psi laboratories and having the opportunity to contribute to remote viewing projects provided me with a sense of balance. My view is that we are all unique. We all have the innate ability to do these things. There has been a wonderful sense of curiosity and excitement in my journey. The future is exciting and challenging. Are we ready?

References

Blackmore, S. 1982. "Have you ever had an OBE? The wording of the question." *Journal of Society for Psychical Research*, June, 51: 794, 292–302.

Section One

CHAPTER ONE

AWARENESS

Prologue to the Phenomenon

As a little girl, about eight years old, I remember being put to bed and "traveling" off around the neighborhood before I went to sleep. I recognized that these experiences were very different to sleeping dreams; I was awake when they happened. I would sit up on the roof and look around or travel down the country lanes of suburban Bristol, in England. These OBEs were spontaneous and random, and occurred without my direction. Later, I was able to bring them under some control.

As I grew older, my feelings were mixed. I felt very self-conscious at the discovery that I was able to do something out of the ordinary, which, until then, I had considered quite ordinary. But over-riding all other emotions was curiosity. I wondered to myself how I would feel if I discovered that these experiences were real, that my impressions could be verified, and that I could accurately describe people, places, and events that I had seen with my mind.

Substantiating the Illusory

I started a program of reading and studying, and found that many well-known people in history had OBEs and that an estimated one-in-twenty people had at least one such experience in his lifetime. About one percent of the population has multiple OBEs. I was surprised at the wealth of literature that was available in the libraries and bookstores.

During the following years I set out to conduct some personal experiments. For example, I would travel to the homes of new friends before I went there physically, to verify my perceptions. I corresponded with other experiencers and we tried to perceive targets that we set for each other. These targets were often as far away as Canada, England, and the United States. The perceptions were not always accurate but enough information was picked up to convince me that the phenomenon was real. During the course of my explorations I also investigated the possibility of using mental travel to explore inner and outer space: looking outward, inward, and upward to discover the past, present, and future; the universe off-world, and the world within us.

The chronology of my experiences was difficult to document because, very often, different types of experience would occur concurrently. For example, a viewing of a current situation might throw up some information related to new technology or a catastrophic future event. During the course of reading this book you will encounter some unusual material referring to dimensions that, until recently, were confined to the weekly tabloid press. A seemingly organized plan of ridicule and criticism has kept such reports from being accepted as a regularly occurring human experience. In Chapter Two I discuss efforts by myself and others to use remote perception to contact and interact with "something" that has been interfacing with human civilization since before written history. Read this material with an open mind. It is possible that we are not alone here, after all.

The Origin of the Journey

Remote Perceptions documents the historic research done by pioneering laboratories in the parapsychological field, in both America and Russia, and how they have provided a basis for future discovery. The work of modern research labs, particularly those prominent in the field are described, as well as the criticisms that have been leveled against their work by the hard sciences and the critical community.

Remote Perceptions has been a journey of exploration; placing my feet and pen onto past, present, and future paths, where others have feared to walk. We are beginning a new era where many areas of study, once thought to be unfit subjects for research, are now becoming legitimate. I began *Remote Perceptions* in a spirit of free inquiry and my hope is that it will add to the increasing respectability and eventual acceptance of remote viewing and its practical applications by the scientific community.

This book began in 1979, as I started learning about my own OBEs, while I was working as a researcher at Manchester University, England, and studying towards my masters degree. While I worked at the university I was entitled to attend courses, and I enrolled in a class called "The Outer Limits of the Mind" developed by psychologist Tony Pritchard.

At the first meeting of this class, about twenty students sat in a circle. We introduced ourselves, and talked about unusual personal experiences. I was astonished. Here were people talking about OBE experiences that I had taken for granted, as if they were something unique. Most of those who talked about their mental travels had isolated experiences through the medium of drugs, alcohol, or trauma such as an accident or surgery. They thought they were privileged to have experienced one.

I sat listening until it came to my turn, wondering what I should say. These individuals, recounting their experiences, felt that each event was very special and unique. If I told the group that I had experienced literally hundreds would I undermine the validity of their experiences? Would they think I was exaggerating my own experiences? Would they think I was weird? These and other thoughts whirled around in my head. Eventually, I expressed my surprise that what they thought unusual was something that I had experienced frequently since childhood. Interestingly, there was another person in the group who had also had OBEs since childhood.

The Phoenix Awakes

After the class finished for the evening, a group of us walked down to the local pub, the Phoenix, where we continued our discussions on parapsychology. That evening was the first of many spent discussing unusual phenomena and formed the basis of several long-lasting friendships.

Gwen and John, an older local couple, were the first people that I talked to after the class and I felt an instant rapport with them. I discovered that John was a textile chemist, who had a keen interest in the investigations of the Shroud of Turin. Gwen, a retired nurse, worked with the homeless. Both Gwen and John studied and practiced a form of Sufi meditation.

Jeff and Kit, a younger couple, were actively interested in all aspects of the paranormal. Jeff worked as a technical engineer at the university, a man with a brilliant mind who could build you anything electrical. Kit, his wife, a petite redhead, studied meditation techniques.

The Teacher Appears

Then there was Vladimir Zakian. At first I was wary of this charming man with the flashing, laughing eyes. I learned he had attended the same undergraduate university, Cardiff in Wales, as I had. There is a saying that when a teacher is needed, one appears. This man captivated me and I became his student in metaphysics. Born of Italian parents, who were then living in Egypt, Vladimir spent most of his formative years on the east coast of Africa, where he spent time with his uncle, an engineer, building bridges in Kenya.

Vladimir lectured in theoretical mathematics at the University of Manchester Institute of Science and Technology and his work in abstract mathematics has been acclaimed as ten years ahead of its time. Vladimir was also adept in Buddhist mediational techniques, which he taught me. Basically, he instructed me in Buddhist "mindfulness" exercises during which the student tries to stay "in the present" as much as possible, both during his meditation sessions and in daily life. I discovered that a flower visualization, that I had developed for myself, mirrored a similar mediation technique used in Transcendental Meditation (TM) training.

During the initial six months of instruction with Vladimir (I studied with him for two years) I was ecstatic at learning new techniques but frustrated that Vladimir did not accept the fast pace with which I acquired new states. For example, during one meditation experience I entered a blue zone of non-being, where no thoughts existed, only intense joy and love. Later I learned that I had entered the state of Samhadi. Vladimir was unable to accept this, stating that it took years of intense training to enter this state. Vladimir also believed that OBEs were part of the oriental Sidhis, or "gifts," that came with meditation; they were to be enjoyed and then left behind as the student progressed. I found that concept difficult to accept, as mental travel appeared to hold so much potential and was an intrinsic part of our humanity.

It was during this time of intense metaphysical training that I had what Maslow called a "peak experience." I was walking from the main campus of Manchester University to the Medical School, and thinking intently. In one, seemingly, split-second I experienced an overwhelming feeling of oneness with everything. There was no connection between "me" and "not-me." I was everything and everything was me. I did not know at the time that what I was experiencing was a state which the mystics call "union with God." Sometimes these experiences are accompanied by perceptions of physical changes, feeling very large or very small, but the overwhelming feeling is that everything is seen in a new perspective. It was overwhelmingly physical, mental, and emotional, all at the same time, yet words could hardly describe the feeling. I tried to express the experience in a poem:

> In one split second in the continuity of eternity
> The mind perceives the workings of infinity
> In Gestalt form all life fits to a pattern
> Creating a whole from isolated fragments
> Carries the perceiver into feelings of humility
> And deeper understanding of the meaning of humanity.

From our discussions at the pub arose the "Phoenix Project," named first for the pub where we met after class, secondly because of the symbolism connecting the rising Phoenix and my mental experiences, and, lastly, because of a Phoenix-like bird that inhabits my sleeping dreams. The Phoenix of my dreams represents the inner mystical and spiritual part of my self. The Phoenix Project had several aims: we wanted to investigate the current state of research into OBEs and, if possible, carry out some experiments to learn more about the phenomenon.

Genetics or Environment?

My growing awareness of my abilities spurred a need to know who I was. It created a conflict within me, a need to trace my roots, to reassess myself, to look at where I came from and where I was going.

I am a typical Anglo-Saxon Englishwoman, now a naturalized American citizen, born in 1946, right after the end of the Second World War. I grew up in war-blitzed Bristol, in the Celtic south-west of England, and saw the city rebuilt and renewed during my childhood. My family, working-class Bristolians, can be traced back for centuries in the village of Shirehampton where I grew up. One branch of our family, the Powells, can be traced back to Stanton Drew in Somerset, where ancient standing stones speak of habitation before the advent of written history. My great-grandfather Frank Saunder's family came from Bratton in Wiltshire, where mystical crop circles have been appearing for the past decade.

I examined my heritage as part of my quest. I was part of the beginning of the baby-boom, born to a British World War II veteran and POW, Ronald James Powell, and a vivacious Bristol city woman, Catherine Joyce Tanzell. Both my parents left school at fourteen to work; my father in a flour mill and later at the Bristol City docks, and my mother as a housemaid. My ancestry was mixed; mostly from country yeoman stock. My great-grandfather, my grandfathers, father, and uncles had all worked at the Bristol City docks. The women on my father's side were the professional achievers: the nurses, the teachers, the managers. I was my parents' first-born child, and I had two younger brothers, Michael, who died in infancy from pneumonia, and Alan, who became my constant childhood companion. Alan suffered from Attention Deficit Hyperactive Disorder (ADHD) and was constantly in trouble. At an early age I took on the care of Alan, because my mother worked and there was nobody else to watch him. We grew up in the Celtic southwest of England, played in the buttercup fields of the Bristol suburbs, spent summers picnicking at Stonehenge, played hide and seek around the stone remains of Roman villas, and felt a pride to be British, despite the poverty that we lived in. Like many post-war English families we lived in City-owned, rental housing and I was always cold as a child. We had no central heating, only a coal fire in the living room. In the winter we had frost on the insides of the windows of our unheated bedrooms. But, even though it was a tough, disciplined childhood, it was a happy one.

I cannot remember exactly when I had my first OBE, but I recollect a lot of experiences when I was about eight years old. However, they could have started earlier and I forgot them. Most of my early experiences were mundane. The OBEs were spontaneous and random, occurring mostly without my control or direction, although I could travel to specific places, if I concentrated. The OBEs usually happened when I was in bed, before sleep, and I realized early on that my experiences were not dreams. I was still awake when they occurred.

One night, when I was about ten, I traveled out of my body to the house of my grade-school headmistress, Wendy Heywood, at Avon Primary School in Bristol. I was upset because she was leaving the school. She was a wonderful woman who had encouraged her students' interest in wildlife and nature, and my talent for writing poetry. I was curious to see where she lived. At her house, in the out-of-body state, I observed many beautiful things, including a lot of crystal and cut glass. The next day I told her what I had seen but called it a "dream" as I had no term to describe my experience. She was amazed at my accuracy.

Mrs. Heywood was aware of my parents' strictness and my extreme shyness and, when I was ten years old, she offered to adopt me. My parents were willing to do this and I was given the choice. I chose to stay with my parents. My mother related that she, too, had almost been adopted. My maternal grandmother had worked for a group of nuns, as a cleaner, and they wanted to adopt my mother. This sounds strange, but in England, particularly in the past, children from poor families were often placed with other families to be raised. It was not considered unusual for a firstborn child to be sent to live with grandparents when a second child came along.

Growing up in post-war England was an adventure. We shopped with food coupons, we made do and mended, and our play was inspired, not by television, but by creative imagination. We became fairies and goblins, knights and monsters; we recreated myths in our childhood play. I even had an "invisible friend," a small ball of light (like Tinkerbell), that I pretended stayed on my headboard at night. Tinkerbell was not of this dimension. Only my mother and I ever saw her, usually at night, and I never saw her in any other form but the small ball of light. We communicated mentally, mostly about the world and its mysteries. She only stayed for a few years and then was gone. My mother, pragmatic as mothers are, told me that Tinkerbell watched over me at night—to keep me safe, like an angel. Not only did Tinkerbell keep me safe but she opened my mind to horizons that are closed to most children. As a young child I became a peace-maker, and a catalyst between many people and many worlds, a role that I still play as an adult. The events that I experienced as a child and young adult spurred my interest in being of service to others as a nurse, social worker, and scientific researcher. They certainly evoked a great deal of curiosity about this world . . . and other possible worlds.

The British, working-class community that I grew up in had a very tolerant attitude towards psychic phenomena. Events which others have termed paranormal were commonplace and normal to us. My mother would ask me to go to the store and I would tell her what she wanted. I would know where my parents were when I needed them. None of this was considered unusual.

I was a bright kid in the working class community where I lived, but being smart was not okay. I underachieved to conform to the expectations of my family and friends, and did not realize I was smart until I left school. During my childhood I was incredibly shy and quiet. I think this shyness was a family trait, as I had a cousin who was mute around adults until her teens. I loved music, poetry and books, nature, the outdoors, and animals. During my teens and early twenties I became very religious and spent a great deal of time in church activities, mainly Baptist and Pentecostal. I enjoyed the exquisite prose and poetry of the Bible. Throughout my childhood, despite my extreme shyness, I was the mediator in many family and social situations, intervening between my rebellious younger brother and my over-cautious parents, between warring classmates, and in street feuds.

Nocturnal Visions

During my early teens, OBEs sometimes occurred during dreams. Each year my parents would take the family on vacation to the south coast of England where we would rent a "caravan," an aluminum trailer, for the week. Alan and I had a great deal of freedom to explore the chines—pinetree lined walks and the sandy beaches. Before one holiday, I dreamed that we had entered a large house on a cliff and descended several stone steps inside the front door into a large inner room. In the center of the room was a circular fountain and pool with goldfish. During the holiday, Alan and I went with Mum and Dad to the Russell Coates Art Museum, which sits up on the high cliffs overlooking Bournemouth Beach. As I stepped down the stairs into the inner room, there was the circular pool, the fountain, the fish. There was an amazing feeling of *deja vu*. I had told Alan about the dream before the visit and I now told him, "Here it is."

Then, when I was sixteen, I went to France on a school trip. We stayed in Paris on the Rue de La Fayette and I was in heaven. I loved Paris. It was exotic, novel, and exciting. Before the trip I had dreamed that I was traveling on a bus in a thunderstorm. The bus approached a large house and we stopped because of the storm. In the large front entrance were alcoves containing statues of gods and goddesses. The dream had a mystical, magical feel to it. During the trip to France, our group did, in fact, take several bus trips out to the French countryside. On one of those trips we got caught in a thunderstorm and an eerie feeling came over me. We did, indeed, stop at the large house, which I recognized as we approached it, and it had alcoves on the inner wall of the front porch. However, these did not contain statues of gods and goddesses, just cushions for weary travelers.

Another time, after I left home, I dreamed that I was on a bus, again, in my home city of Bristol. A neighbor, Mrs. Lloyd, got on the bus. She looked young and vibrant, not the old lady that I knew she was. She said she wanted me to know that she was okay. The next day I received a note from my mother, with an obituary notice for Mrs. Lloyd, who had died a few days before. At the time, these dreams amazed me but I didn't take them too seriously.

Exceptional Human Experiences

Growing up, and for most of my life, I have experienced telepathy, clairvoyance, out-of-body-experiences, psychokinesis, and precognitive impressions. Experiences like these have been termed Exceptional Human Experiences or EHEs, by Dr. Rhea White of the EHE Network. Rhea has been collecting such experiences to establish their relevance. I saved the life of two little brothers on the same day by listening to an inner impression that warned of danger. I was able to pull one child out of a swimming pool, and caught his brother as he fell off a playground slide. At the time, I was working as a social worker intern at a children's home in southern England. The two brothers, a wild 4-year old, Jack, and his mute 2-year old brother, John, were at the institution because their mother was in prison. One morning we took several of the children to a local playground. The other social worker, Marianne, and I sat at the bottom of the slide catching the children as they slid down. There was a lot of laughter. Suddenly, I had a visual impression of the younger brother, John, tripping on his shoe as he came down the slide, falling over the side and onto his head. Following my impression, I got up quietly and stood at one side of the slide. As John started to came down the slide, his shoe caught the edge of the slide and he fell sideways, right into my arms. Later that day, I got a visual image of Jack, with his arms and legs straight out, floating in water—an event that happened in the late afternoon, that day, as the children were swimming in the pool. One minute Jack was there with the other children, then he was missing. I "knew" what had happened and was able to fish him out, unharmed. I often wonder what became of the brothers in later life.

During my nursing training, I realized that I had the ability to heal others. I would anticipate patients' needs before they asked and I was able to soothe very sick babies by holding them. In 1973, I had the opportunity to work as a nurse/social worker with a British voluntary organization, VSO, at an orphanage in Colombia. Here, severely malnourished babies, who were also socially and emotionally deprived, were rescued from local institutions. We set up a remedial program for those infants and small children. We hugged, rocked, and sang to the babies. We hugged them, tickled them, and took them for walks and other exercise. We also hung up colored posters and mobiles, and played music to them. These babies, that had been written off as unrecoverable, thrived.

Most of the orphans were adopted into American homes and I have been following their development for more than twenty years. These young adults are graduating high school, starting jobs, going into the services, attending college, getting married and having babies of their own.

Precognitive Puzzles

In my pre-teens I became frightened of my abilities. Sometimes the experiences became precognitive. In my innocence, I thought that, maybe, I was causing the events to occur. Before going to sleep at night, I would go on mental adventures—looking at events in the world. Sometimes, I would see tragedies happening—car crashes, houses burning, people dying, all in great detail, as if I were actually there. Then, I would read about these events in the next day's newspaper. Not knowing that what I was experiencing was a form of precognition, I felt that I was playing some role in these tragedies. It felt terrible and I curtailed the nightly excursions. Perhaps these early experiences sensitized me to the hurts of the world and served to shape my helping role in society.

I cannot recall having any further travels until my teens, when they became very intense and spontaneous. They would occur at very inconvenient times: when I was in church, praying, or when I was waiting for a bus. Although I was a religious teenager, I did not think of OBEs as a gift from God. In fact, if one occurred during prayer I would feel it was wrong to go floating off.

Unfortunately, I didn't document my travels during those early years but wrote poetry which reflected my experiences. I was a quiet, studious teenager who took life very seriously. I wrote about my feelings, about life and its mysteries. I would lie awake at night watching the moon and the stars and later I would write poetry about my thoughts. The most frequent OBEs during this period were of the observer kind, where I would travel to an unknown place and look around. Sometimes I would watch people—a boy catching eels, soldiers in a cave, or sailors in a storm.

One of the first things I did after the first meeting of the Phoenix Project group was to sound out my family about unusual personal experiences. This was a tricky task. I wondered if they would think me strange? My probing revealed that neither of my parents had similar experiences and their attitude was one of tolerant skepticism.

However, my father's sister, Auntie Marge, had experienced a Near-Death Experience (NDE) during surgery for the removal of a tubercular lung. She heard the doctors talking during the operation and later confirmed that her observations had actually taken place.

My biggest surprise came when I questioned my brother, Alan. He told me that his experiences didn't start until he was seventeen years old but he remembers us talking about my experiences when we were children. His experiences started when he smoked what he thought was marijuana and later found out that he had been smoking opium resin. He had an extreme psychic experience during the opium intoxication and, from then on, experienced OBEs. Alan told me that during his experiences he often visited our parents' house in Bristol, and my home, at that time, in Manchester, England. Our parents were usually asleep when he visited but he said the cats recognized him.

Prior to a Christmas visit to Bristol in 1977, Alan's skeptical wife, Julie, asked him for proof of his abilities. So, he took a mental trip to a spare room at our parents' home. The room had recently been decorated and he described how he stood in the darkened room and saw the street lights shining through floral patterned curtains. Later, when Alan and Julie were in Bristol, they were given the spare room, but Julie was quick to point out that the curtains were plain. Later, however, when they put out the room light, the street lamps revealed a floral weave in the apparently plain curtains.

When Alan is traveling in an altered state he says he often meets other people who appear quite ordinary and are fully dressed. He usually travels to the countryside or to houses of friends or relatives. He adds that the people he sees in this state usually greet him, and he thinks that they are people who are also having OBEs.

Like me, he has also been above the earth and looked back with awe and wonder. He is able to initiate spontaneous mental travel but only has the experience occasionally. He is fully conscious during the trips and, like me, can choose his destination. Our experiences are similar in that he usually feels very tired when he returns to the body. In May of 1979, I possibly caught a glimpse of Alan terminating a mental trip to my home in Manchester. I awoke to see him standing by the wardrobe in my bedroom but, as I looked, the image faded away.

Recreating the Cosmos

In my twenties I felt more secure in my mental travels to go further out from my body. In my mind, I had been quite far from home and on various trips around the world, but I felt a curiosity to go further. Each time I took a mental journey I would go out a little farther from the earth. I was scared, in case I could not get back. It was an exhilarating experience to see the Earth from such a distance but I was disappointed that I could not see the individual countries as clearly as on my school globe. It was all a big, beautiful blur. When television began showing news of rockets and astronauts going up into space, I felt quite smug knowing that I had seen it before them. Another time, away from the earth, I visited a place where there was a lot of water, it was very blue, had very little gravity, and smelled of ozone. I still have no idea where this was.

Marital Misfortunes

In my early twenties I married for the first time, just after I graduated as a Registered Nurse, and married for all the wrong reasons. I saw older, single nurses, bitter in their spinsterhood, and decided that I did not want to end up like them. So I married the second man who asked me. The first marriage proposal came from a black, Italian doctor at the hospital. My extremely conservative parents forbade me to see him and I, dutifully, obeyed their wishes.

The man I eventually married was older and divorced, and turned out to be physically and verbally abusive. In the short course of our married life, he often accused me of adultery where none existed, slapped me while I slept, split my lips with his punches, threw me down the stairs, and even tried to choke me. Even though my family had been strict, I had never experienced such violence. When I complained to my mother-in-law she commented that this was "what women should expect from marriage." I eventually left my husband and got on with my life.

Meditations in the Midlands

So, here I was in 1989 in Manchester following graduation with a bachelor of science in psychology, from Cardiff University in Wales, and working towards my masters degree. We all have watersheds in our life—this was mine. At times I felt that I was moving too fast—other times too slow. For a time I felt like I had lost my sense of self but the rigorous demands of my research position did not require personality, only an objective awareness of the here and now. I watched and recorded the behavior of my subjects as I watched and recorded my own. During this time I recorded my dreams and my daily meditations, and noted episodes of Kundalini energy that brought with them an increasing mind/body awareness.

During times of great stress the OBE ability disappeared, only to reappear during more tranquil periods of my life. This goes against the psychological theory that these experiences are an escape from life stress. Later, while I was abroad, many thousands of miles away from home, I would "travel" home to Bristol.

In late 1978, during my metaphysical training with Vladimir Zakian in Manchester, I decided to try and direct the destination of my travels and visited Vladimir's house. When I asked him later about the house (which I had never physically visited), he confirmed that there were two doors to the left in a hallway, leading to a front room and a bathroom. There was a closet to the left of the hallway, about halfway along. The corner room at the top, left of the hallway, was a living room, and the stairs were to the right of the hallway. I was able to confirm these facts when I physically visited the house.

Also in that same month I mentally traveled to the apartment of a friend of Vladimir's. I saw the room in detail and had the impression of a stuffy atmosphere: a musty, non-aired smell. I confirmed my perceptions with Vladimir and he said that the room was arranged as I had described it. He also confirmed that the room did have a musty smell; it was the bachelor apartment of a psychology professor friend at the University.

Metaphysical Manifestations

During these mental trips I would try to move things and try to read, but I could do neither. There was only one time when I was able to look back and see my body, and, unlike other adepts, I have never seen the silver cord that is supposed to attach the astral body to the physical. Historically, the concept of the silver cord was encouraged by the Theosophy movement. According to Carlos Alvarado, OBE researcher at Edinburgh University, the concept of the cord was also carefully maintained and kept alive by experiencers, such as Muldoon (who was very influential), and later writers such as case collector Robert Crookall. Perhaps some individuals need the presence of a silver cord to remind them of their connection to the earthly realm. In occult literature, when the silver cord breaks, then death is supposed to have occurred. Maybe death is the ultimate out-of-body experience?

In March of 1979 I traveled to a place where it was autumn. I was high up on a hillside surrounded by trees in autumn foliage. I was walking along a dirt path, enjoying the beauty of the leaves. To the left I saw three lakes—two small ones, and one large. They made the shape of a fish, and I "knew" that the combined lakes were called "Fish Lake." I walked along looking at the hills. Small rivers ran into and out of the three joined lakes. I thought that the place might be in Canada.

There was a monument in front of me and I walked up to it. It was a huge stone seat and I realize it had been made by early people. The stone seat had a mystical, religious significance. Its back was made of one huge stone, carved on the back with religious symbols such as fishes, moons and stars, and letters which I couldn't understand.

Another interesting OBE occurred on a sunny day in April 1979. I was at my parents' home in Bristol, in the garden. It was the first hot day of the year and I was wishing that I could be at the beach, enjoying the sunshine. Then I realized that I could go there mentally. I landed on a deserted beach. It was very warm and the sand was hot and dry to the touch. I was lying, sunbathing, on a sand dune and I could hear the waves rolling onto the beach. Then, I was getting too hot, so I ran down through the hot sand and into the cool sea. I waded in and swam for awhile. Then I came out and sunbathed again.

After about three-quarters of an hour, when I had enough of the beach, I came back to my body and I had no more desire to go to the beach; I felt as if I had already been there.

When I returned to my body after an excursion in August 1979, I stayed outside of my body for a while and tried some simple experiments. I had read that people in the OBE state might be able to produce raps on furniture in the room. So I approached a wooden table and tried to rap on it but, to my surprise, my hand went through the table and I was not able to make contact with it. This was before I read of Robert Monroe's efforts to do the same thing—with the same results.

Researching the Literature

It is believed that about one in twenty individuals experiences at least one, if not more OBEs during a lifetime. About one percent of the population have multiple OBEs. One of the first sources I encountered of such anecdotal material was Muldoon and Carrington's *Phenomenon of Astral Projection*. Not only do they carefully document more than ninety cases occurring under many types of situations (including projections at time of accident or illness, those produced by drugs and anesthetics, and by hypnotic suggestion) but also spontaneous projections. I was fascinated by the wealth of material contained in their work; their bibliography spurred me on to further reading. However most of their references were unobtainable through the usual sources and I realized that I would have to do my own literature search on the subject.

The next source of anecdotal material that I found was the work of Dr. Celia Green of the Oxford Institute of Psychophysical Research in England. In her fascinating book *Out of the Body Experiences*, I read details of the experiences she had collected from the public via an appeal through the press and radio. The Institute received approximately four hundred replies, and about two-thirds of these responded to a questionnaire. The narrative material she collected revealed that many people experienced single or multiple OBEs in a multitude of situations. Green termed these "ecsomatic states." In an earlier paper "Ecsomatic Experience and Related Phenomena," she surveyed a group of undergraduate students at Oxford University and showed that thirty-four percent of the students polled had at some time had an "ecsomatic experience."

In Lyall Watson's *The Romeo Error*, I found a listing of famous people who had experienced OBEs: William

Wordsworth, Emily Bronte, George Elliot, George Meredith, Lord Tennyson, Arnold Bennett, D.H. Laurence, Virginia Wolf, Bernard Berenson, John Buchan, Arthur Koestler, Ernest Hemingway, and Lyall Watson.

Psychologist Kenneth Ring has evaluated the incidence of OBEs, and connected them to other phenomena such as NDEs. He found that about thirty-seven percent of those people he surveyed felt that they had experienced separation from their physical body during an NDE. Ring concluded that perhaps an OBE is an integral part of the NDE. He was fully convinced of the reality of OBEs and their involvement in the separation of soul and body after physical death.

Astral Travels and Astral Doings

My search led me to many and varied sources of rich material. From each publication I learned about new avenues, which I could follow, and I gradually built a small but adequate library. One of the more interesting facts that I learned during my reading was that there is a difference between being "out-of-body" and having an "astral projection." For many years I thought they were the same thing and I would often confuse the two terms. However, I discovered that during a regular out-of-body state, the individual perceives himself to be in a physical world, which closely matches his real world. During astral travel the perceiver feels that they have traveled to other places, sometimes described as the "astral realm," where they are able to see and interact with "astral or spiritual entities." The majority of my purposeful OBEs have taken place in the physical dimension but my brother, Alan, has traveled extensively in the astral realm.

Pragmatic Applications

In Colin Wilson's, *Strange Powers*, I read more about D. H. Laurence's experiences. I was also pointed in the direction of Ingo Swann, a New York artist who recorded his experiences in his paintings; and to the writings of businessman Robert Monroe, who, sadly, passed in the spring of 1996. While plowing through the literature, I was amazed at the multitude of names given to the phenomenon of mental travel. At first I thought that each was a different phenomenon but, when I read the literature, each had a basic definition; the ability to experience something leaving the body, that could exist separately from the body, and view events distant from the body.

During the summer of 1980 I decided that as an exercise I would try and remote view the vacation residence of my friends Gwen and John. I knew that they were in Norfolk, on the east coast of England, but did not know their exact location, nor did I have any pre-knowledge of the hotel in which they were staying. Gwen and John confirmed some of my impressions, which I related to them. Near that time I was lying in bed at home listening to Bach's Brandenberg Concerto on Radio 4, one of my favorite pieces of music, when my "other body" became restless, got up and danced in the middle of the room, in sheer joy, to the beauty of the music. It was a wonderful experience.

In the summer of 1979, the Phoenix Project Group decided to carry out some preliminary experiments. The group decided that I would try and project to the homes of two pairs of group members. As we had recently become friends I had not visited their homes physically, and they had deliberately not talked about where they lived. I was told that in both places there was something distinctive: if I could detect these characteristics, there might be evidence of something paranormal happening.

The next day I called one of the couples and told them my impressions and what I had perceived. I was told, disappointingly, that most of my impressions had been wrong. However, the main characteristics which they had decided on—that at Kit and Jeff's house the color of the bedroom was predominantly red, even the walls—was correct. At John and Gwen's house the main characteristic was that they had lots of pottery items and I perceived this correctly. One of the items that I saw at their house, a tribal mask, was accurate. John had had African masks hanging in the living room but they were so fierce-looking that they had been taken to John's study upstairs because they had frightened visitors.

Although there were many misses in these initial experiments, they served a dual purpose: of practice in controlling the destination of the remote perception; and training in reporting and documenting what I saw. From the end of 1979 onwards I kept a series of journals. After every session I would take time to record what I had seen and heard in the OBE state, even if it was to an unknown place, in the chance that I could later corroborate it.

The Psychophysical Institute, Oxford

Between October 1979 and April 1980, I began to put my subjective experimentation on a more professional level. I contacted a research organization in Oxford, England, the Psychophysical Institute. Dr. Celia Green and Charles McCreery were actively investigating and documenting paranormal phenomena, including OBEs. On five occasions I remotely viewed the Oxford Institute and tried to perceive objects there. On the first occasion I was successful in locating a small storeroom at the top of the house, which I saw as dark and dusty and filled with boxes. This was confirmed although other perceptions were wrong.

The second trip was also successful as I was able to perceive a small room containing only a small table and chair, a test room. On the third trip I was able to perceive that the stairs in the building were white and in the process of being painted. I also saw a sun hat hanging on a wall, which was confirmed, but there were many other observations that I did not get right.

The fourth and fifth trips were not at all successful in terms of identifying specific objects, but from these trips I deduced that the Institute appeared to be a regular house used for scientific research. Although these mental trips to Oxford ended due to lack of further impetus and funds, they served to encourage me to conduct further study and research into the phenomenon.

While these series of personal experiments were often discouraging because of the misses, they were also encouraging in that, throughout, I was constantly working on ways to increase hits. Later attempts brought much better results. Most of my experiences from mid-summer 1979 to early in 1981 were concerned with personal exploration and experimentation.

Almost Full Circle

In 1981 I left England to move to the United States of America, which was to become my adopted home. Prior to emigrating, I carried out two sessions to try and project from England to the United States. I saw the house that my future husband, Randall (pseudonym), was about to move into. Along one side of the house I saw a long pantry. When I finally got to the States and saw the inside of the house I was able to verify that the long pantry off the kitchen did exist. During another brief session to this same house, after Randall had moved in, I saw him working in his home office. In a letter he revealed that most days he had been writing in his new study.

At the time of my marriage I felt that things were wonderful. I loved Randall and the children, and felt that I was loved too. To understand the situation we need to look back to 1973. During that time I was working at the Paraiso Infantil Orphanage in Colombia, South America. I worked for the British equivalent of the Peace Corps, Voluntary Service Overseas (VSO). At the orphanage I had nursed and nurtured severely malnourished and deprived infants and children who were orphans. One of these was Daniel. Abandoned by his mother, a 15-year-old maid, at six weeks of age, Daniel was brought to the orphanage for care and eventual placement in an adoptive home. As I fed and cared for him I would ask "I wonder who your parents will be?" A professional couple came to visit the orphanage and chose Daniel. His adoptive parents, Randall and Susan (pseudonym), were teachers. During the month that they spent in Colombia completing the paperwork they needed to take Daniel home, I came to know them fairly well. They seemed joyous at bringing Daniel into their life. The new family returned to the States and I corresponded with them, as I did with many of the other adoptive families. Randall and Susan honored me by making me a godparent to Daniel. In 1975, I returned to England to work as a residential social worker in a group-home setting in Bristol.

When Daniel was a toddler, Susan became pregnant. Their happiness was shattered by the diagnosis that Susan had lung cancer. Following the birth of their daughter, Sara, Susan went back into the hospital and died. Randall wrote me a twelve-page letter expressing his grief and anger.

When Daniel was about four years old and Sara six months, I traveled to the States from England to visit Randall, and we fell in love. I had to return to England to complete my bachelor's degree, but Randall and I continued our romance long distance. At Christmas 1980,

Randall and I became engaged. He had recently taken over the pastorship of a small Presbyterian church in New Jersey and the congregation welcomed me into their family. In the New Year I had to return to England to complete my immigration paperwork and, despite a lot of red-tape, I returned to the States again in March, and Randall and I were married. Daniel was the ring-bearer and Sara was a beautiful flower girl. Following the wedding Randall made arrangements for me to adopt both Daniel and Sara.

Sadly, I discovered that Randall was also physically and emotionally abusive and the marriage broke up. What saddened me incredibly was that he took Daniel and Sara to live in another state and he only permitted me to see them, occasionally, from then on. Without financial resources I was unable to fight in the courts for my rights as an adoptive parent.

Following the breakup of my marriage to Randall, I continued with my OBE practice and most of my experiences were directed and controlled. However, during a spontaneous OBE in 1984, I visited an area north of New York City. I glimpsed sunlight reflected off water, and the sun just about to descend below the horizon. There were dark stormy clouds in the sky. About a couple of hundred feet below me were mud flats interlaced with pools and waterways, glistening with the last rays of the sun. It was an engrossing, beautiful scene. I didn't descend to the flats, instead I stayed aloft and traveled east before returning to the body. There were many such spontaneous OBEs, scattered throughout the directed ones, that seemed to symbolize my becoming whole again.

Letting Go of the Past

Those were the saddest parts of my life. The remainder has been a wonderful, joyous, exciting adventure. I have traveled all over the world, to Africa, to Russia, Europe, and South America. I met a wonderful man, David Smith, who believes in both partners being supportive and caring for each other. If there is anything to the concept of the soulmate—he is mine.

How we met is an interesting story. David had been in a sixteen-year marriage but was preparing to become single again. He had put out an affirmation to meet someone like me, who would understand his intuitive and creative interests and abilities. Back in New Jersey, I had also made positive affirmations to meet a partner like Dave; someone who would not be threatened by my intelligence or intuitive abilities, and who could be a true partner. I was fed up with being mother and therapist to the men I was dating.

In 1992, I relocated to Las Vegas to work as research coordinator for the Bigelow Foundation. I had decided to give myself six months in the area to get established in my new job, before I got involved socially. However, the first night in town, I met David at a social gathering. Two weeks later we were dating, and, now five years later, we are married and I am stepmom to his boys.

There was another amazing coincidence attached to meeting Dave. While I was at Princeton Engineering Anamolies Research Laboratory (PEAR), I was aware of the remote viewing work being done by the military at Fort Meade. I knew some of the names of the people working at this unit but, of course, this was all held in the strictest confidence by the PEAR lab personnel.

When I came to Las Vegas and started dating Dave, I mentioned to him that I have been doing consulting work for a group called PsiTech, which was a business comprised of ex-military remote viewers. Dave mentioned that his oldest brother, Paul Smith, was also doing remote viewing. The next time that I talked to Ed Dames, head of Psi Tech,

I mentioned that I thought I was dating Paul Smith's brother and asked if he knew Paul. Ed thought it was too much of a coincidence but checked anyway; and yes, the two Paul Smiths were one and the same. It makes one wonder whether the cosmos has a plan for us and how much free will we really have?

Paul served for seven years in the military's remote viewing program at Ft. Meade (from September 1983 to August 1990). During 1994, he became one of only five government personnel to be personally trained as coordinate remote viewers by Ingo Swann at SRI-International. Paul was the primary author of the government RV program's CRV training manual, based on Ingo Swann's work. Paul is credited with more than one thousand training and operational remote viewing sessions during his time with the unit at Ft. Meade. His training program, Remote Viewing Instructional Services (RVIS: Austin, Texas) is a small, newly-created company whose mission is to train individuals in the theory and practice of Coordinate Remote Viewing (CRV).

Last summer, I was privileged to be included in one of Paul's basic CRV classes and found that the training greatly enhanced my ERV training. In addition, it has been an honor to have Paul as a friend and brother-in-law.

It has now been twenty years since I began researching and documenting my experiences. It has been an exciting and often breath-taking journey of discovery. The phenomenon is real. We can access information about distant locations and events. Being able to do this does not distract from who we are. The fact that we can do this makes us, in fact, more whole.

For many years I wanted to be seen as "normal." I denied my abilities, particularly in front of my academic and professional colleagues. It is the beginning of a different era. A paradigm shift is occurring. Perhaps now we can acknowledge ourselves as whole beings: physical, intellectual, emotional, spiritual . . . and intuitive.

References

Green, C. 1967. "Ecsomatic experiences and related phenomena." *Journal of the Society for Psychical Research.* 44: 733, 111–131.

Green, C. 1968. "Out-of-the-body experiences." *Proceedings of the Institute of Psychophysical Research.* Vol. II. Oxford, England.

Monroe, R. 1971. *Journeys out of the body.* Garden City, New York: Doubleday.

Muldoon, S., and H. Carrington, 1969. *The phenomena of astral projection.* London: Rider & Company.

Ring, K. 1984. *Heading towards omega.* New York: William Morrow.

Swann, I. 1977. *To kiss earth goodbye.* New York: Dell.

Watson, L. 1974. *The Romeo error. London: Coronet Books.*

Wilson, C. 1975. *Strange powers.* London: Abacus.

CHAPTER TWO

LOOKING OUT

Inner Outer Space

Since I was a small child I have had a fascination with outer space. I followed the activities of Leica, the first dog into space, and the launching of Sputnik with the same fascination that some kids follow rock stars. When Yuri Gagarin became the first man into space, I stuck the newspaper cuttings up around my room until my mother made me throw the yellowing scraps away.

Many times, in my childhood and teens, I would travel up above the earth to look down on the world. It was a wonderful, awe-inspiring experience. In the spring of 1983 I decided to see how far I could go away from the Earth; in March and April I remotely perceived the planet Jupiter.

Jupiter Probes

My reason for doing these trips was that I had read that a NASA space probe called Galileo would evaluate the atmosphere of Jupiter in 1988. There, the probe would encounter intense heat and pressure, up to twenty times that of earth, and intense cold. Temperatures range between minus 243 to 145 degrees Fahrenheit above zero. The probe would test air pressure, temperature, composition of the atmosphere, cloud density, net radiation and amounts of hydrogen and helium in the Jovian atmosphere. However, the Galileo probe was not launched until October 1989, and did not reach Venus until 1990.

In the past, remote viewers, such as Ingo Swann, have attempted to do their own mental space probes, and their perceptions have closely matched the later, actual findings. So, I decided to do my own probe of Jupiter in March and April of 1983, record my observations, and then, eventually, compare my observations with those of the Galileo probe. I also decided to send my observations to the American Society for Psychical Research in New York for them to hold on record. The report was also sent to NASA's Jet Propulsion Laboratory. The viewing took place on several separate occasions between March 6th and April 3rd, 1983:

1. During the first attempt all I could perceive of Jupiter was a mauve-purple haze. Perhaps I didn't get close enough to the surface?

2. I went to the outer atmosphere of Earth and looked at the curve of the Earth, then went out to Jupiter. I went through the purple haze and landed, to my surprise, up to my neck in water, which I hadn't expected. The shore was composed of some kind of quartz, which I thought at first was amethyst, but realized was the clear rock surface reflecting the purple atmosphere. I wondered why the water was not frozen or evaporated with the extreme changes in temperature. It was thick and oily, and I had the insight that it could change its molecular structure to avoid freezing or boiling. There was no sign of human-like life.

3. I decided to go somewhere else on Jupiter and arrived on top of a range of exquisitely beautiful mountains composed of a quartz-like crystal reflecting the purple atmosphere. They were at

least as tall as Mt. Snowdon in North Wales. Although the mountains were made of quartz, they were not transparent.

4. There were what I thought fields of very tall, purple grass, only to find that the "grass" was also composed of quartz. I don't know if it was "growing." It bent and waved like fields of long grass, yet it was also like looking at a sea of sparkling waves. It was beautiful.

5. Leaving Jupiter I came back to Earth and saw the west coastline of Europe very clearly. I traveled north to see the south coast of England and flew in close over the patchwork quilt of little fields. I flew east until I came to the United States and back to my own body.

Unfortunately, delays set the timetable back for Galileo to reach Jupiter and the probe only recently entered Jupiter's atmosphere, thirteen years after my initial remote viewing. Although all the data has not yet been analyzed, it is interesting that one of the findings is that Jupiter has more water in its atmosphere than originally estimated.

Space Junk

In September of 1983, I decided to go outside the Earth again. I had some initial difficulty getting out of the Earth's atmosphere this time, but I managed it in stages. I looked to see if I could see any satellites. I reasoned that there should be some around, above the earth's atmosphere. I saw a man-made satellite, made of metal. Its center part was a cylinder, the size of a washing machine drum, but longer and a bit narrower. It had a single round lens at one end pointed at the earth. Extending on either side of the satellite were arms, each arm was three times the width of the satellite. The arms were composed of small girders, criss-crossing. At the end of these arms were spoon-shaped antennae which were able to rotate.

In January of 1984, out of curiosity, I decided to go out above the Earth again to see what was there. I saw the Earth about as big as an orange held in front of your face. It was lit up by the sun but had a sort of haze around it, like the corona that you often see around the moon. I decided to go further out and saw the moon by the Earth and the Earth itself about the size of a quarter. I turned and looked out to space: it was empty, vast, and eerie. It made me want to return to the haven of Earth.

Around the Earth I found a tremendous amount of junk. I saw something like a metal cog, about the size of a steering wheel of a car, made of metal with a hole through the middle and notched teeth round the rim. There was also a shaft or axle about four or five feet long, metal, and chunks of stone. I was surprised as I thought that everything burned up when it entered the Earth's atmosphere. I also saw pieces of irregular-shaped sheet metal, a conical form, black on the surface and hollow, and large, metal ball bearings. Such incongruous items to find floating around in zero gravity. Although most of my mental travels had been Earth-bound, these purposeful OBEs assured me that human consciousness is not tied to the Earth, but is free to travel away from gravitational restraints.

Zero Rads

During the summer of 1994 I decided to try a different type of mental travel (combined with psychokinesis or PK) in an effort to possibly neutralize radiation. These experiments were done in a spirit of scientific inquiry and not for any political or social reasons other than to explore the potential of the human mind. I formulated some questions and answers before going ahead with my experimentation.

1. It has been shown that the mind can affect the outcome of a radioactive source (Schmidt, PK experiments). I watched a TV science documentary, *NOVA*, on parapsychology and read the commentary. Several physicists, using controlled techniques, found that both men and women could affect small amounts of radioactivity mentally. These results were replicable. I felt that there should be some way that the mind could affect radioactivity on a larger scale, but it had not been attempted to my knowledge.
2. There should be no effect on the individual because only the mind is being used as a catalyst. The effect on the environment should be minimal, if only a small amount of the total radioactivity were affected.

On July 4, 1984, the Saturday following that, the next Wednesday, and on several occasions after that, I tried to create a "negative radioactive balance" in various civilian locations with no success. I thought that I would hear some news in the media, but there was nothing. I felt I should get more specific and refine my efforts.

On the morning of August 19, 1984, I tried to neutralize radioactive sources in locations on the west coast of the United States and in central Russia and was so exhausted afterwards that I slept most of the day. The effort could have two effects: to knock out computers, and neutralize radioactivity.

I felt that I was successful in the United States as I mentally perceived cries of protest from the computer personnel while I was viewing the site. They immediately suited up and went out to check their gauges. In Russia, there was a similar outcry but a different reaction. The computer personnel went to play cards and await work crews to fix the computers and check the gauges.

On August 26, 1984, at about 3:40 pm, I attempted another experiment and I got a similar reaction. In the United States, the computer personnel were very angry and cursing. I tried to perceive the gauges and saw zeros. In Russia, the computer room was empty but the area around the gauges was crowded and noisy.

On September 22 and 23, 1984, I tried two final attempts for this series of experiments. The locations this time were in mid-Washington State and mid-west Russia but I did not get any feedback from the locations. Disappointed by the futility of these experiments I discontinued them and put my efforts into something more productive.

Perceiving Glitches

On August 30, 1984, the news media announced that the launch of the shuttle Discovery was halted because of "glitches." I decided to go and have a mental look at what could be causing the problem, which seemed to be mainly concerned with computer software; but, of course, had no actual feedback on my attempts.

In January, 1986, the shuttle Voyager launch was delayed for about five or six days. I decided to go see what the problem was. I found a small screw blocking the F15 fuel line, which could not be seen from visual inspection. I tried, unsuccessfully, to convey this information to the shuttle personnel. However, the following day the media announced that a "bolt" was found blocking a "fuel valve."

On February 9, 1986, after the terrible Challenger disaster, I tried to view where the remains of the bodies might be located, as the media announced that searches were underway. I visited the location, in Florida, on two occasions: February 8 and February 9, 1986. The black astronaut was trapped by his left arm in deep water by a large clump of rock and weed. He had moved location within the bay. To the side of the bay nearest the light-house was the nose-cone, black and triangular, in shallow water. It was resting on the sandy bottom and lit by sunlight.

The female astronaut, Christa, was in very deep water off the coast and lodged between layers of cold and warm water like a sandwich. I thought that she would eventually drift ashore but this would take months and the body would not be recognizable. The remains of the others astronauts were widely disseminated. *and did?*

you report this? to whom? result?

Consulting for Psi Tech

In the late 1980s, I was recruited by a small group of ex-military researchers who had been trained by the army in a practical application of remote perception, which they termed remote viewing or RV. I was not then trained in the strict protocols they used, but the group, Psi Tech, headed by Major Ed Dames, felt I had sufficient ability to participate in some of their projects. I used a form of viewing called extended remote viewing, which included several altered state of consciousness methods. Over the following few years I provided coordinate remote viewing data on several projects for Psi Tech, which was then located in Virginia.

The Rings of Saturn

In the early 1990s, Psi Tech split up, and at least two separate groups were formed: Psi Tech relocated to New Mexico; and Intuition Services was formed in California. I was commissioned by Intuition Services to undertake a remote viewing of the rings of Saturn. In his book, *Ring-makers of Saturn*, Norman R. Bergrun shows pictures of "immensely large, enormously powerful extra-terrestrial space vehicles, located in the vicinity of Saturn and its moons." Intuition Services requested a remote viewing of the rings of Saturn to possibly verify Bergrun's claims. I deliberately did not look for or read Bergrun's book as I did not want to influence the viewing. After two unsuccessful attempts to approach Saturn through the rings, I approached the planet from a vantage point a few thousand miles above its "north pole," and viewed the rings as a flat circular area. From this vantage point I was able to view the various elements of Saturn, its rings and planets.

Report to Intuition Services

Intuition Services provided a set of questions for guidelines, as follows:

1. Are there natural phenomenon that would account for bright luminous light sources in the rings, or in the vicinity of Saturn?

(a) There are some very bright "hot rocks" circulating in the outer rings that have been attracted by the intense gravitational pull of Saturn. These rocks are both thermally and atomically "hot." They circulate in the outer rings for varying periods of time while their constituent elements are broken down and distributed, according to their degree of breakdown, between the rings.

(b) Also in the outer rings are unmanned anomalous craft. Within the inner rings are vehicles that have been captured by the gravitational field and are in various stages of disintegration.

2. Are there rings that are incomplete? If so, how did the missing ring segment disappear?

The main factor that describes Saturn is "cyclic." Due to its intense electromagnetic pull, space debris is constantly, but erratically, attracted to the planet. This debris initially rotates in the outer rings and undergoes a process of degradation, then the various elements are distributed among the rings according to degree of molecular "weight," much like a gas spectrometer which distributes elements in a banded strip, except in the case of Saturn the strip becomes circular. Because of the random and irregular nature of the space debris that is pulled into the gravitational field, the rings fluctuate in their completeness and cycle from open to closed along both their length and width—the rings are not uniform in their density. This cyclic nature of the rings is dictated solely by the nature and amount of debris that enters the gravitational field.

3. Describe the nature and origin of the planet Saturn? How will the planet evolve and eventually die?

Saturn evolved from a collection of electrically charged rocks that became attracted to each other and formed a nucleus. Gradually, as the mass became more magnetically powerful, it attracted an increasingly greater number of similar elements. These initial, charged rocks may have come from an earlier Saturn-like planet that became too "over-charged" and disintegrated. This may possibly be the fate of the planet we now know as Saturn. We tend to think of Saturn as static but it has a decidedly cyclic and dynamic nature.

4. Describe and sketch the number, size, and orientation of unusual anomalies in the rings of Saturn?. . . and 5. How long have these anomalies been there and what is there main mission or goal?

Active within the outer rings of Saturn, and inactive within its innermost rings, are numerous, immense, metallic, tube-like unmanned craft that are basically mining vehicles. They are hollow internally and space debris flows constantly through the interior. This debris passes through many sheet-like fields which act as transparent membranes that sort the various elements before they are attracted and degraded by an internal collection and storage ring, which is off-loaded periodically. These mining craft are silent and non-mechanical. They are powered by a very small amount of the elements they collect and the overall yield of these mining operations is a tiny fraction of the incoming collection and does not contribute significantly to the cyclic density of the rings. These craft have been here for at least the last hundred years and possibly long before that. It is difficult to date the craft. Occasionally, a large "hot rock" will enter the mining craft and destabilize its function. The inactive craft within the inner rings are mostly casualties of this accidental process and are basically left to disintegrate to their constituent elements.

6. Why have they chosen Saturn and have they explored other planets of our solar system?

Basically, Saturn is an enormous, concentrated resource of raw elements and this is the main reason the unmanned craft are in place. Periodically, other unmanned craft come to unload the yield. The craft that are seen within the region of Saturn and its moons are dedicated craft, whose sole purpose is the mining of elements from these areas. They have not explored other planets of our solar system. The area was chosen by an intelligent species that directs the mining operations that have explored other planets of our solar system including Earth. This tall, thin, humanoid species, which is pale, smooth, and hairless, inhabits an underground/underwater region on Titan where they are able to enter semi-fluid (mud-like) surfaces. They live in cold, underground areas, which contain a great deal of moisture. The walls are metallic but resilient to the touch.

7. What, if any, relationship, do the ETs working the rings of Saturn have to do with Earth?

Very little. The ETs operating the mining activity in Saturn's rings are aware of Earth as a potential mineral resource. However, its populated status, and the fact that the majority of the Earth's minerals are not easily accessible, deters the ETs from active interaction with Earth. Earth has been extensively mapped and explored by this species. However, it is far easier for them to access the concentrated resources of Saturn.

8. Is this a cooperative intergalactic/inter-civilization alien activity in the rings? Or is it just one race or group?

This is basically one race or species. However, they have knowledge of, and have interacted with other groups. The intergalactic term is a human-generated concept and does not apply to the majority of those groups outside Earth. There are some groups that have formed some sort of mutual coalitions but an all-encompassing intergalactic cooperative is not evident from this viewing. Other ET groups have explored and mapped the rings as a potential resource.

9. What makes the rings of value to these people?

An easily accessed source of concentrated mineral elements that are needed for manufacturing, medicinal, and other purposes. It is possible that they may also trade off some of the yield. The use of unmanned mining craft ensures the safety of the operation for the ET species and the loss of an occasional craft is expected.

10. Are the gaps in the rings natural or created by the extraterrestrial intelligence?

No. The gaps in the rings are the effect of the cyclic nature of the rings themselves and the debris that they attract. The amount that is mined is negligible and cannot account for the gaps in the rings. Gaps will continue to occur and close in the rings at cyclic periods.

11. Are any of the moons of Saturn operating as ET bases? If so, which ones?

Only one, the sixth, Titan. The eighth, Phoebe, may have been used at one time, but a natural disaster caused it to be abandoned as a stable environment.

12. Describe any new currently undiscovered aspects about Saturn that modern Earth science would find important.

A rich resource of readily available raw minerals, including several new elements in combination. This combination could have potential as a new form of lightweight alloy. I am not sure if this has already been manufactured by Earth science.

The group was very excited by this last answer and scheduled several more sessions regarding the new elements' manufacture and qualities. As the group is currently patenting this new information it is not prudent to publish it here, but groups interested in becoming involved in its manufacturing and testing should contact Intuition Services.

Unusual Personal Events

As I undertook these new and exciting explorations I wondered how many other people there were who had the same experiences and what characteristics they shared in common. Psychologist Kenneth Ring has found that people who have experienced "unusual personal events" in their lives, such as an NDE or seeing a UFO, also share an increased perception that they have experienced such psychophysical events as expanded mental awareness and "information flooding." In *The Omega Report*, Ring describes the personal experiences of these subjects, which include OBEs during childbirth, surgery, and other traumatic events. However, whether these experiences occur because of these stressful events or whether the events trigger an already fantasy-prone personality, is a debatable question.

In 1991 the Roper organization polled the American public to evaluate the occurrence and distribution of certain unusual personal experiences. The resulting *Roper Report*, "Unusual Personal Experiences," presented the combined data from three national surveys of nearly 6,000 adult Americans. It was the collective effort of Professor John Mack of Harvard Medical School; Dr. David Jacobs, a historian at Temple University; Dr. Ron Westrum, a sociologist at Eastern Michigan University; Dr. John Carpenter, a psychiatric therapist in Missouri; and Budd Hopkins, artist, writer, and researcher from New York. The Report was mailed to nearly one hundred thousand psychiatrists, psychologists, and other mental health professionals across the country. According to the Report, the surveys concerned the relationship between unusual personal experiences and what the researchers called the UFO abduction syndrome.

One of the indicator questions concerned the feeling that the person had left their body. The poll respondents indicated that fourteen percent of them had, at some time or another, felt that they had left their body, and four percent of the population polled said that this had happened to them more than once. Interestingly, a proportion of executive/professional and white collar workers reported more mental events than other occupational levels. This group, identified by the Roper organization as the "influential Americans," reported the greatest number of OBE events. This group also answered positively to four or more of five key indicator questions in the poll, suggesting that they may possibly have had other anomalous experiences.

The Roper Report has generated a great deal of criticism from the scientific community. However, the figures stand by themselves to indicate that not only do a great number of people experience paranormal experiences, but that the number increases with education level and social activity. This goes opposite to the popular idea that people who have these unusual experiences are uneducated and socially gullible.

The Demise of the Mars Observer

In August of 1993, NASA's Mars Observer was on its way to view the Martian surface when it suddenly and inexplicably went dead. No communication was heard from the Observer after its system was shut down in order to pressurize the fuel tanks. As an avid computer bulletin board system (BBS) "lurker" I followed reports of NASA's efforts as they tried to communicate with the errant craft and get it back into communication.

The UFO community, particularly Richard Hoagland's group had suggested that NASA may have deliberately sabotaged the Observer to prevent further pictures of the famous "Face on Mars" from being filmed. There were wild speculations that NASA had secretly turned the Observer back on and that pictures of Mars were being relayed to a secret location, where clandestine surveys of the Martian surface were being carried out. In a radio broadcast at the end of November, Hoagland made a prediction that the Observer would suddenly regain communication by January 8th or 9th, 1994. However, January came and went and nothing happened.

One day on the BBS, a correspondent made a tongue-in-cheek comment about "Where are the remote viewers when you need them?" I took up the challenge and e-mailed on August 24th, to the BBS contact at NASA, and gave him the following remote viewing of the crippled Mars Observer: When the fuel tanks were pressurized a small escape route (shaped like a small cat door), which allowed excess pressure to escape but not return, got stuck. A small particle of grit caused the malfunction of this small door and because it could not be completely closed it caused a domino effect that prevented the device from coming back on-line. It is possible that repressurizing the device could dislodge the grit and cause the door to fully close. This would trigger the proper sequence to bring the device back on line.

However, I wonder if anybody at NASA will be listening by then? I recently read Courtney Brown's remotely viewed scenario of the demise of the Mars observer in *Cosmic Voyage*, and our two versions do not correspond. Basically, Brown says the Martians did it.

When I sent my report to NASA, I figured that they would think I was a "flake" and would not even respond. I was wrong. That same day they e-mailed back, thanking me for my input and commented that there were a number of possible scenarios that they were considering as the cause, including something close to the one that I had described.

In January of the following year, NASA released a report from the committee that had been studying the Mars Observer and its loss of communication. They had decided that the most plausible scenario was that fuel valves had leaked as the Observer had made its way to Mars and this condition had aborted the sequence of events that would have put the Mars Observer back into communication. They also commented on the need for security and cleanliness during pre-launch activities indicating that some debris had been implicated in the failure of the probe. NASA estimated it would be late in 1996 before they retrieved the Observer and nobody would know the actual cause of the loss until then. As of July 1998, this has not been achieved.

CSETI and Coherent Thought Sequencing

In December of 1993, NASA decided that one of its projects, the Search for Extraterrestrial Intelligence or SETI, had become an unnecessary expense to the Agency and cut the $12 million dollar funding to this group. SETI had been involved in the monitoring of the cosmos for signals that might indicate the existence of other intelligent life forms in the universe and had already had promising leads (the "WOW" signal) although no conclusive results. Prior to the budget cuts SETI had changed its name to the High Resolution Microwave Survey, in an attempt to portray a more scientific image.

Now, SETI has turned to private funding sources and has managed to raise $4.4 million of the $7.3 million needed to keep them functioning. Another name change has taken place and the group is now known as the SETI Institute headed by Frank Drake. The SETI project has been renamed Project Phoenix.

During the time that SETI was going through this internal turmoil another small group, headed by trauma center physician Steven Greer from Asheville, North Carolina, calling itself CSETI, (Center for the Study of Extraterrestrial Intelligence), was becoming established. CSETI is dedicated to facilitating and documenting CE-5 UFO encounters. That is, conscious, diplomatic interaction with UFOs and their occupants.

Greer defines CE-5s as close encounters which are caused by intentional human action: for example, flashing car head-lights at a UFO. A first degree CE-5 occurs when the interaction brings a craft into the vicinity, and a secondary CE-5 can occur when a craft is already in the area. To achieve first degree CE-5s Greer and his working teams employ lights, sounds, and a form of remote viewing called "coherent thought sequencing." Sometimes, to achieve high-quality interactions, RMITs (Rapid Mobilization Investigation Teams) are deployed to an area where notable sightings have already been recorded.

Working on the principle that the occupants of the craft utilize non-verbal communication, such as telepathy and remote viewing, Greer holds training workshops where these skills are learned and practiced. To date, the team has reported significant interactions in England and Mexico, as well as in the States. For example, in southwest England a team meditated during the night near fields where crop circles had previously appeared. Although no craft were seen that night, they discovered the next morning, in the field behind them, the same design that the group had meditated on during the night.

Although some of CSETI's goals, such as preparing parties for boarding a landed craft, seem premature, and the group's use of paramilitary language and tactics seems unnecessary, they have been successful in establishing a link between humanity and whatever or whomever is visiting our skies. On a lesser scale, I, too, have been working to establish this kind of link.

Meeting of the Minds

It began in England in 1962. When I was sixteen and my brother Alan was thirteen, we lived in the rural heart of Dorset, in southern England. We had a unique experience that initiated a train of unusual happenings and generated a host of intriguing questions. The search for answers to these questions has taken me across international, social, and cultural boundaries; into bookshops, libraries, universities and colleges; into research and support groups; and to many seminars and conferences. I now have many key pieces to the puzzle, and can start to see that the picture on the "puzzle box" is one that has been seen by many thousands of experiencers. That picture is of a small gray humanoid with large, dark eyes, pointy face and an oversized cranium.

That spring night in 1962 was not unusual. My brother and I talked about the day's events, school, holidays, friends. Our bedrooms were at the back of the house, facing a long country garden where my mum and dad grew vegetables and roses, a row of old elms, a brook, and a country meadow. Suddenly our rooms were lit by an incredibly bright light. I became very frightened and hid under the bedclothes. My brother, a braver person than I, looked out of his window and said that a UFO had landed in the meadow and that there were people walking around. My brother watched for some time and occasionally I would ask, "Are they still there?" and he would reply, "Yes." As suddenly as it appeared, the light went out and they were gone.

Following that night I suffered from terrifying nightmares in which I would squeeze through many small spaces before arriving at a long gray room. There, at the end of the room, was a box-like table. I would experience the most incredible terror. I would wake from these dreams in panic. Although I searched, I could not find any event that could account for such terror. Ever since that time, strange events continued to occur, perhaps related to the Dorset event in 1962.

Finally, in 1993, after years of personal memory and dream search, I decided to undergo some professional hypnosis sessions. I had assumed that if anything had happened that night in 1962, it would be revealed during hypnosis. During the sessions I recalled the light, then I remember there being five of us in my bedroom and the room being filled with golden light. Alan and I, and three beings were involved in a five-way communication which occurred without words. Disappointingly, I cannot recall what the interaction was about. What I do remember is that Alan and I were not frightened of these tall, golden beings. In fact, there was a feeling of belonging, of being taught important things, of somehow being given a destiny.

A Different Kind of Contact

During the active, interesting years that followed, similar strange events continued to occur. I was at a loss to explain them, so I put them aside. In 1988 I attended a scientific conference at Cornell University hosted by the Society for Scientific Exploration. After the day's scheduled talks, a small group of researchers convened in one of the residences to discuss the UFO/Abduction phenomenon. I was professionally intrigued by this topic, which examined the concept that some people claimed to have been abducted by aliens, subjected to medical examinations, and caused to suffer from an amnesia that hid their experiences from themselves and others. According to researchers, notably Budd Hopkins and David Jacobs, hypnosis could uncover the hidden memories and lead to an understanding of the phenomenon.

I had talked earlier to one of the researchers, Richard Haines, and related the Dorset incident to him. He suggested that Alan and I may have been witness to an anomalous event. I did not want to hear this.

At the evening meeting, one of Dick Haine's projects was to show the group a series of slide illustrations of aliens that he was collecting for a projective test. Sitting in the corner of the room, I watched the slides with an increasing nervousness that developed into a full panic attack. My heart started thudding. I could not breathe, my legs shook, I felt giddy, and I wanted to run out of the room screaming. This was so unlike my usual character; people call me Mary Poppins because of my calm, capable personality. Part of my mind was denying the panic, saying "This is all nonsense. There is absolutely no need to feel this way. It is all imagination." Another part of me, amazingly even calmer, was telling me that I had better take notice of these feelings, as there could be something here that needed to be explored.

Initially, I determined that I did not want to undergo hypnosis. I did not want someone else determining what was real or not about something immensely personal that I desperately did not want to be real. I decided to gently explore my inner self through dream recall, a personal memory search, meditative journeys, journal keeping, sharing and networking with other people who had similar experiences, and reading everything related to the subject. I was determined to face the phenomenon and steal its thunder, whether it turned out to be a new undiagnosed form of psychosis, an interface with another dimension, an unknown manifestation of group consciousness, or a hard, nuts-and-bolts reality.

Later, I joined several professional organizations dedicated to understanding the phenomenon and got caught up in the crossfire between two abduction researchers battling by letter-writing, each intent on promoting their approach to the problem. I got caught up in the paranoia of suspecting governmental authorities of being actively involved. Whenever I queried abduction researchers on the state of the field, all I got were offers to hypnotize me.

The terminology they used ("abductions," "aliens") assumed that the phenomenon was extraterrestrial, and a totally negative experience. I decided that I would refer to my experiences as "interfaces" and to the entities as "visitors." Until I could understand the visitors' intentions, I could not assign a negative or positive quality to their interactions.

When I finally decided to tell people about my experiences, I found that I was ignored. This was actually a relief as I thought I would be ridiculed, or maybe even fired from my job. It was also sad, because as a competent researcher and experiencer, I could help throw some light on the subject. I continued to read the many—often ridiculous—theories surrounding the phenomenon, to monitor the infighting between groups supposedly helping "abductees," and to watch the exploitation of the experiencers.

A Jigsaw of Events

During the past seven years, I have been adding data to my information pool, finding new pieces to the jigsaw as new information links with the old. I have gone through intense pendulum swings of belief ranging from outright denial to full acceptance of the phenomenon's personal and global significance. Reading everything, watching the media, talking to other experiencers, attending talks and conferences I continually add information to my mental database on the topic. This information is then shaken down through my "reality filter" and I see what drops out and what matches up. It is surprising what "noise" can be filtered out in this way and amazing what links up.

Three Roper polls have indicated that perhaps five million Americans may have had experiences very similar to those claimed by UFO abductees. I believe this population varies in its reaction to the experience. In any random population, a small percentage will cope poorly. Often, experiencers will present with symptoms that are diagnosed as post traumatic stress syndrome (a psychological reaction to an overwhelming traumatic situation). I believe that individuals from this group were the ones that initially sought out the early researchers of the phenomenon and how "abductions" came to be seen in such a negative light. Another small group will bring good coping mechanisms to bear on their experiences, and perhaps will not seek out therapy. Over the past few years I have been very fortunate in belonging to several groups of professional people who are well-established in their own fields and who have found ways to integrate their anomalous experiences into their daily lives.

Data Downloads of a Mysterious Kind

The details of my own interface experiences have already filled twenty, ongoing journals and are too numerous to write about here. Part of me is hesitant to write about my interface experiences. They sound bizarre and unreal to someone who has not experienced them. However, I am finding that I am not alone in reporting, for example, the teaching sessions, where we have been "downloaded with information." Most of these have occurred in the dream state; but one of these took place, during full-consciousness, when I was 16 years old, while walking in the English countryside. While walking, my mind was pondering on life in general, nothing profound, just everyday musing. Suddenly, as if a window had opened in my mind, "information" streamed in. Most of this information was beyond me; I could understand just a fraction of it, which related to my previous musing. It was as if a child had asked how a TV set worked and someone had given the child a crash course in advanced communications electronics. At the time, I was rather religious and thought that God had given me the information. I said,

"Thanks, God, but that's much more than I needed." I was so awed by this experience that I never told anybody until a few years ago.

Another time, I was lying in a reverie on my bed trying to take an afternoon nap. Suddenly, across my visual field, scrolling very fast from right to left, was a banner of golden light containing small, dark images. Accompanying this was a high-pitched vibration in my right ear. It was frustrating to watch this banner of light moving so fast that I could not read the images. Fully conscious at this point, I concentrated hard and was able to slow down the scrolling of the banner. It contained small black symbols, some of which I understood, and most that I didn't. The images were a composite of glyphs that I had seen in mystical writing, runes, and many symbols that I had seen only in dreams.

Unidentified Flying Objects

All my life I have wanted to see a UFO: not just a light in the sky, or a fleeting glimpse of metal, but a real, honest-to-goodness structure. Both my parents had seen them; my brother, Alan, had seen them; and so had most of my friends. I joined the Mutual UFO Network, hoping to hear of places to see them, or techniques to see them better. However, the only unusual flying object I ever saw, appeared to be a probe of some unidentified kind.

The Appearance of the Rub Tub

It appeared one February evening, as dusk was settling over Princeton, New Jersey. I had a ride home from work with a friend and we had been chuckling about a colleague who had ordered rubber tubing from the stockroom, writing his request as "Six Rub Tubs." (We eventually named our sighting as the "Rub Tub" in his honor.) As we approached Harrison Street, from a side street, we saw what looked like a large soap bubble bobbing about eighteen inches above the road. It crossed the road in front of us, looking as if it would pop any second. It was perfectly round and was iridescent, like a soap bubble, but it didn't wobble or change shape like a bubble. My friend saw it as faceted. We turned onto Harrison, watching the "bubble" bob along on the other side of the street. Then it stopped and made a ninety degree turn up a driveway. Up to this point we had been amused and curious, saying, "What is that?" When the "bubble" made the right angle turn, we got out of there as fast as we could. I have since talked to others who have had similar experiences, and who feel that the "bubble" might be some kind of ET probe.

Solid Illusions

On at least two occasions, other-dimensional entities have taken on a physical reality. One night, when I was living in Princeton, I awakened on the staircase to find myself with a small, grey entity—the type with the large head and large black eyes. In the twilight, I could see him a few steps above me. He put his face very close to mine and I was holding his little, thin neck, trying to hold him away from me. He was very strong. In my frustration, I bit his head. It felt like hard rubber—no bony skull, just yielding material. In the morning I felt dreadful remorse and wished that I could have handled the interface in a less aggressive manner. I got another chance.

A few months later, I awoke to feel the bedclothes being pulled softly from me. I was fearful and did not want to open my eyes. I knew I was awake. I put out my left hand and felt a small entity standing close to the bed. I put my hand around where its waist would be. There was no waist, just straight up and down, firm and rigid. It was standing straight and still, with its arms at its sides. A companion stood at its right: I could hear it "whistle-piping." I sensed that they were both distressed. I communicated, mentally, that I did not want to harm them, and I received the same communication back. This was one of the most profound experiences of my life.

I could have ignored my contact experiences, if it were not for another woman who also saw the visitors. Mary (not her real name) was visiting and I gave her my bedroom, while I slept on a futon in the adjoining living room. I had not told Mary of my experiences. In the morning, she asked if I had seen anything unusual in the bedroom. She described how she had woken in the night to find two "gargoyles" standing in the middle of the carpet, in her room. One was facing the short corridor to the living room and the other was facing the window opposite the bed. A brave soul, she asked, "What do you want?" Immediately, they turned, then vanished. She was quite shaken, and so was I. Until then I could dismiss my contact as a dream or imagination—now it seemed very real.

Confronting the Monitor

One of the ways that I have learned to cope and understand this phenomenon is by actively trying to view the entities involved. I must point out here that I am not a channeler. I do not relay messages heard from disembodied spirits. What I tried to do was to directly access the source of my own interfaces, to find answers for myself. In 1991, over a series of purposeful remote viewings I made contact with an entity, whom I will call the Monitor, because of this entity's search for knowledge about the human race. A log of each meeting follows:

February 25, 1991. Open Interface One

Decided to request a mental interface with the "visitors" with several aims in mind:

1. To exchange information
2. To understand goals, and
3. To achieve mutual cooperation.

At first I conveyed "Request Information" and "Request Interface" following a meditation period. However, I realized that those terms put us on an unequal standing and changed my thought to convey "Interface Open" to indicate an openness for dialogue. I visualized myself before an open window through which an interface might take place and sensed interest and curiosity but nothing happened.

Then I found myself in a woodland scene, it was summer, and sunlight was streaming through the tall trees. I didn't understand at once, then I realized that we were meeting on neutral territory. It was if we had to create a virtual meeting place that was neither theirs nor mine, although it did resemble an English woodland.

I walked through the woods and sat on a stone seat and waited. From out of the woods came "the wise one" or Monitor, very wrinkled, and slightly stooped. We exchanged looks and each of us held out a hand. I decided to be honest and told the entity that his hand reminded me of a chicken claw and was repulsive to me. He (assuming a male gender) responded that, to him, my hand was just as repulsive. This got us off to a good start.

He asked whom I represented and I replied that, basically, I only represented myself, but indirectly represented many other people, both in close circles of friends and wider groups. But the decision to interface was mine alone. His reply was that he represented all of his kind, not that he was above or better than others, just a representative.

We agreed that there should be a sharing of information and a statement of goals but we would have to decide what information and what goals. This was easier for him as there was already a consensus on what could be represented by him. I was at a disadvantage as I spoke initially for myself but indirectly for others, a process totally different from theirs. We did decide that there should be mutual cooperation and that we should return to discuss other topics.

At this point I was feeling exhausted and I decided to close the window—it was taking a great deal of energy to maintain the interface. However, it was agreed that the open window would be a signal to indicate openness to interface and we would meet again in a neutral mental setting. Some information would be given and translated by means of their technology and the entity and I would interface again when the next opportunity arose.

February 26, 1991. Open Interface Two

At 10 pm I entered a mediative state and visualized "Open Interface" as an open window. My mind wandered onto mundane thoughts about my work as I waited but my attention was brought back to the Monitor standing on his side of the window. He came to my side of the window, into a virtual room. He stood and I sat. I asked if he wanted to sit. He replied that sitting and lying down were human actions. He asked me why we had not adapted, over the centuries, to gravity and still had to counter its force by sitting. I replied that I did not know. We agreed on the first of several ground rules:

1. We would each do what was normal for us: He would continue to stand and I would sit if I wanted. We would not expect the other to conform to our idea of normality.

2. We also decided that we would be honest, even to the point or risk of offending the other. This way we could learn without false pretense.

3. The Monitor said that my opening the dialogue was one-sided and that he should also have the opportunity to initiate open interface. At first I commented that this might not be convenient but realized how unilateral this was and agreed that we should both have the opportunity to initiate dialogue.

4. It was agreed that communication should be telepathic; sometimes in the form of reciprocal dialogue, sometimes in picture form.

I said, "Where shall we begin?" to which the Monitor replied, "We have already begun."

When we had only been interfacing for about five or ten minutes, I said that I was tired and wished to end the interface. The Monitor responded that I was being unreasonable by calling him to interface for such a short time. I explained that I was tiring and that it was an effort for me to interface. I was basically multitasking; being in a meditative state, trying to keep some vigilant facility to dialogue and think, and trying to remember the dialogue in order to record it correctly. This was energy-draining.

We agreed to close the interface and try again another time. Perhaps it will get easier with practice. However, I felt comfortable that we had been able to lay down some ground rules which are mutually agreeable. Although it seemed as if nothing major was accomplished I still felt that these two interfaces had been successful preliminary stages.

February 27, 1991. Open Interface Three

I had decided not to initiate an interface but perceived the Monitor requesting an interface at 10:35 pm. So I meditated and opened an interface. We found ourselves in a lighted globe. The wise one had a companion and requested that I bring another person to interface. I explained that this was not easy—telepathy was not a strong characteristic of humans. I would have to arrange an interface through physical means, for example the telephone. However, I tried to contact my friend Paula telepathically. I requested her to interface with us and I felt that she was present (wearing a purple warm-up suit). However, the contact was not maintained. The companion to the wise one remained quiet.

We talked about our different concepts of time as objective (linear) as well as time as subjective (holistic). The Monitor could accept holistic time. He asked me to describe clocks. I began by saying that clocks were devices for measuring time and took many forms. The earliest, easiest ones were just sticks in the ground, measuring the shadow of the sun as it passed overhead. The Monitor queried, "But you are just measuring the passage of the sun, not time." I tried to explain the notion that when the sun passed from Point A to B, that interval was accepted as a measure of a unit of time. There was a similar dialogue regarding clocks: "They are only measuring sound," and I used the same argument in return that the interval between tick A and tock B was agreed upon as a measure of time. There seemed to be little acceptance of the concept of linear time—I almost said that the concept was alien to him.

This third interface presented two new issues:

1. The expectation by the Monitor, as a representative, that more than one person could interface but the realization that it is easier for them than for us; and

2. Concepts of time and its measurement are different for them and for us.

At this point, I think we both realized that we had only covered the surface of our queries. I started thinking about some personal things towards the end of the session and the Monitor abruptly terminated the session by stating "Interface closed." There was no reproach or anger, just a decision to end the dialogue until the next time.

Unfortunately, the next week I suffered an accident which resulted in a cut hand that became infected and I did not have the emotional reserves to continue the sessions. However, I do plan to work with several local meditation groups here in Las Vegas to see if a group approach to the Monitor yields any interesting interactions.

Communicating with the Cosmos

Other researchers, such as Professor Courtney Brown, in his intriguing book *Cosmic Voyage*, have also tried to understand the phenomenon by attempting to communicate directly with the visitors. Courtney Brown was trained by Major Ed Dames (ex-military remote viewer). Brown calls his version of remote viewing scientific remote viewing (SRV). *Cosmic Voyage*, while being ostensibly a book about remote viewing, covers the topic of extraterrestrial life; and more specifically, two types of entities: the Martians and the Greys. I like many of Courtney Brown's quotes on the validity of remote viewing; that it is a statistically tested skill and a reliable research instrument. He also brings in recent corroborative research materials and papers. *Cosmic Voyage* is a record of Brown's training with Psi Tech.

Regardless of whether or not humans can remotely view extraterrestrial life, what can be acknowledged is that the altered state of consciousness can be used to access information about the cosmos outside of our earth. Being out-of-the-body during these excursions is one of the greatest experiences that humankind can have. Consciousness freed from the limiting confines of the physical body must be similar to what astronauts experience in a gravity-free environment.

Mysterious Area 51

How would you access information about an area of land that was not even supposed to exist? Through remote viewing maybe. Many people have asked me if I have remotely viewed that controversial area of the Nevada Test Site, named Area 51, also called Dreamland. I can respond honestly that, yes, I have viewed Area 51 but there wasn't really anything too exciting there. The following is a report of a viewing that I did in the fall of 1992, at the request of the Bigelow Foundation. As I had some idea of the kind of terrain the area was situated in, I decided to look for unusual activity in and around the location.

There was some activity up in the far northwesterly corner where I saw dynamiting and explosions occurring in the mountain side. There was activity to excavate into the hillside in order to build part of the facility underground or under the hill. Most of what is on the surface of the area, such as hangars and outbuildings, are only partially functional; most of the activity is underground.

I did not find any live Extraterrestrial Biological Entities (EBEs) but there was file evidence that they had been there, both dead and alive. They are no longer at the area.

I did see some fascinating engineering projects. There were the standard v-shaped aircraft but with an upwardly-curved back, like a lateral arch on the back surface. There were also half-circle crafts with this same arched, curve in the back. They looked like horseshoe crabs. There were a few bat-shaped crafts which had two arched curves cut into the back surface.

Where's the Roswell Wreckage?

About a year later, in April of 1993, I was asked to do a viewing by Intuition Services to locate the whereabouts of the Roswell wreckage. (It has been widely speculated that a UFO crashed in Roswell, NM in 1947, and that the event was covered up by the government.) The group wanted to know the current whereabouts of the wreckage and to locate a paper trail that could lead investigators to information regarding a possible Roswell cover-up.

As usual the group supplied me with a list of non-leading questions to which I gave the following answers:

Report to Intuition Services

Current Time:

1. Where is the majority of the Roswell crash wreckage now? Where is it being studied now?

Large pieces of triangular and strut-like pieces of debris, wrapped in green cloth (surgical drapes) and over-wrapped in tarpaulin are sitting on dusty shelves in a warehouse at Wright Patterson Air Force Base. They are very high up, to the very end of row S. This row is the farthest right as you enter the front entrance to the warehouse. The warehouse door is open to the light and, currently, not closely guarded. People come and go through the open door.

There is an office space to the left of the front door (as you enter) and all the itinerary of the warehouse is coded in a locked file cabinet. In the cabinet are references to documents located in a locked file in a two-story stone building on the base. Documents there are dated 1958 and are yellowed with age around the edges. They relate to physical examination of the debris. The documents have a decal on the top left, of a circle with a horizontal stripe through, and writing is superimposed on the design. The debris is not currently being studied, but there is renewed interested from Los Alamos.

I did not see any round (flying-saucer shape) debris. When Brazel reported the debris to the military and they issued the initial press release, the debris that Brazel found was reported as a "flying saucer." This was purely a case of misinformation and confusion brought on by people not communicating clearly. Immediately, it was assumed that a round-type UFO had been discovered, and sparked all the conjecture and stories that followed about the finding of a UFO. There was no round debris from the Brazel incident, and therefore nothing to study.

There were one or more non-human bodies found near the Brazel ranch and these were removed immediately after they were found. The finding of these bodies caused a great deal of panic and anxiety, miscommunication, misunderstanding, and general chaos.

At one time, the bodies were "lost"; they had been rerouted by accident to another military location but were eventually recovered and studied. There was paperwork prepared for the removal of the bodies (at least two), but they indicated that the remains of two dead airmen were being moved. The names given were something anonymous like John Doe and James Doe. There was a rumor around that the bodies were of German paratroopers that had lain undiscovered after their plane crashed during the war.

2. Describe any living civilians that were aware of the crash before the military arrived. Male/female? Age? Occupation?

Besides Brazel and his family, and people who have been described in the literature and in the media, there were two other people who had knowledge of the debris. One was a young boy, maybe a nephew, who was at the ranch shortly after the crash. There was also a young woman, a friend of the wife (housewife, wife of a neighbor) who was shown the debris. She didn't say anything because the wife showed it to her without Brazel's permission.

3. Is there a private source who has proof of the early July 1974 crashes? Describe that person and his home.

There were various surgeons, pathologists, and medical personnel, with military connections, who were sent samples of biological tissue and debris to analyze after the crash. One such person is a heavyset man with a florid complexion who lives in the New York area and works in New York City. He has several homes, including one in Westchester County.

4. Is there important documentation to be found about the crash in non-secret vaults, such as government archives or presidential libraries? If so, which ones?

All the important documentation related to the crash is still in secret vaults and not available to the public, yet.

5. Are there other crashed UFOs on the planet that have not been recovered that could be? If so, where are they?

Yes. Peruvian Andes, Colorado Rockies, Russian Urals. Round shapes have been recorded on spy satellite images of the Rockies but have been dismissed as anomalies or geological formation. Maybe the mountainous areas cause crashes due to misjudgment of height, weather conditions and geomagnetic anomalies. Despite their advanced technology, the craft pilots do make mistakes.

Early July 1947:

1. What caused the crash(es)?

An electrical storm combined with fluctuations in the electromagnetic field of the earth, that is, an electromagnetic anomaly in the geography around the Brazel ranch.

2. Describe the aftermath and activities of the personnel around the crash site at the Plains of St. Augustine, NM and at the wreckage area near the Marc Brazel, Foster sheep ranch.

There was a great deal of anxiety and confusion, miscommunication, misunderstanding of orders, dereliction of duty, reporting sick and general disturbance among the military personnel. Nobody knew what anybody else was doing, orders were given and rescinded, personnel were ordered to one location, then told to return as soon as they got there, a general feeling of incompetence and confusion.

3. Were there live or dead non-humans at each site? Where are the corpses now? Are they or were they actively studied by humans? If so what are/were the surroundings? What are/were they studying? DNA structure?

At least two non-human bodies were found. Cell structure was studied as well as morphology. DNA wasn't discovered until 1953 and by then the bodies of the aliens had been cremated. (The bodies got so disgustingly putrid after thawing for tissue samples that they had to be burned.) The testing of the tissue samples did not take place in one location but was sent out to multiple labs. The individuals doing the testing were not told the specific source of the samples, just to analyze them as a biological sample and make a report.

Sometime in the Future:

1. Is there a key witness or document that will "break open" the Roswell case in the future? Please describe the document or the person. What is the color of the markings at the top/bottom of the document?

Wings. Blue. The Manager of the Wright Patterson warehouse has been there a long time and knows what is on the shelves. Maybe when he retires he will be willing to give information.

Solitary Isolation

In the course of doing the above viewing, I recounted some information relating to another underground location. There is an underground facility (probably in Nevada) where one or more live aliens might be located. They are in an area built from concrete. There are two rooms both accessed from a corridor running down the right hand side of the rooms. The corridor slants downwards and leads to rest rooms and utility areas. The first room is an observation room and has an angled glass window that overlooks the lower, second room. The back of the first room is full of computers and monitoring equipment. You have to go up two steps to get into the first room as it is raised up above the level of the second room.

The lower second room is permanently lit and contains the aliens. They are in there with nothing more than a round wading pool of water. There has been one by himself, at times, and the emotion that I feel from this creature is of extreme isolation. They are live creatures and do not survive well alone. Occasionally, adult humans come to try and communicate with the aliens but until now there has not been much success and the aliens have died. Surprisingly, there has been a steady "capture" of aliens over the years, mainly of the gray variety.

The Four Corners Incident

On January 12, 1994, an incident occurred which was noted and followed by NORAD for a week. The event caused a great deal of concern in the Four Corners Area of New Mexico.

A large thermal signature was noted by tracking satellites and a large fire was suspected but when the area was checked there was nothing to be found. In August 1994, Intuition Services commissioned me to do a remote viewing of the site and provided a list of questions that required responses per their protocol.

This remote viewing investigates the "NORAD" incident which started on January 12, 1994 at 2:55 PM and continued for about a week. The location of the incident is 37 degrees 30 minutes North Latitude and 106 degrees 18 minutes West Longitude. Following are my responses based on a remote viewing of the event:

Report to Intuition Services

Preliminary viewing: A planned, staged event. A covert operation.

1. What caused the large thermal signature that NORAD detected? Did it pass into the earth, or crash killing the occupants? How did the event end?

What NORAD detected was not a thermal signature, but it was interpreted by their technology as "thermal" because of its unusual nature. There was no crash, no occupants killed, and the signature originated at several hundred feet above the surface. The signal was an interaction between a new energy technology and known electromagnetic signals already being generated in and around the area. The signal was generated and registered by a set of three towers set in a triangular, or trigone, pattern set about a hundred miles apart.

The energy produced a plasma, amorphous in shape, and spread over patchy areas of about fifty to a hundred miles. The concept was similar to Tesla's original idea of long-distance energy transfer. The event ended by the signal being turned off so that the results could be analyzed. The event may have been detected at night by the appearance of apparent lightning, when no storms were evident. The lightning appeared greenish or bluish.

It is possible that people in the area biologically detected the energy and suffered from minor conditions such as headaches, ringing in the ears, stomachaches, and peripheral neuritis—pins and needles in the hands, feet and limbs.

2. Is there an underground military or ET base in the sighting area? If so, what is its purpose and function? Describe the size of the base and the access procedure to the base from someone walking.

There are underground bases but not in the Dulce/ET sense. The bases are strictly military and designed to access satellite information and to detect and analyze military activity. Access to these sites would be difficult as most are accessible either by air or by heavy four-wheel drive vehicle. Some are on reservation land or military land (covert use) but one or two could be reached by walking. They are not readily recognizable by eye, but look for new plant growth over heavy vehicle tracks. Most of the bases are small, usually only one- or two-story deep, and their primary functions are tracking and accessing satellite or radar information.

3. Did the helicopters searching the area a few days later find anything interesting? Were they really US military helicopters or just images that appeared that way?

A variety of craft were sent into the area, both small airplanes and helicopters, military, government, and civilian. None found anything unusual although a few reported instrument disturbances of aircraft controls.

4. Is the incident of November 30–December 1, 1993, in the La Garita area associated? Is so, how? Was there a crash? Any recoverable hardware evidence?

Sorry to disappoint you but no, no, and no. The incident in the La Garita Area was the result of a natural phenomena, local talk, and exaggeration. The incident did not cover such a large area as the 1994 incident and did not generate as much attention.

5. How many active and inactive ET bases are there in Colorado and New Mexico? What is the purpose of the inactive bases? What is the mission of the active bases?

There are no actual ET bases (as described by the UFO community, such as the one at Dulce). Ets appear to come and go regularly but do not appear to have established a permanent site as a base. There are favored touch-down places such as lakes and mesas.

6. Are there joint US Military and ET bases? What is the purpose of such cooperation? Describe the nature/scope and specifics of any technology transfer that occurs at these underground bases.

There are at least two bases, not underground, on apparently inactive military sites, which house at least one occupied UFO each. One is housed in a large building, which has steps up the side, which lead to a side door, onto a walkway inside which looks down onto two large rectangular pools of water. In one is a saucer-shaped UFO. ETs of the slender grey variety are able to enter and exit the craft more easily and the water pressure (providing buoyancy) prevents internal damage to the ship and the occupants when they are inside. There are rooms to the side of the larger building where ETs and humans can interact for short periods. There has been an exchange of information and both humans/ETs are learning about each other. Some of the ETs agreed to wear human clothing when interacting with the humans to facilitate psychologic acceptance by the scientists and civilians that come into contact with the ETs.

7. Has there been any active misinformation given about the NORAD incident? If so, what is the falsehood and why?

As it seems with most government agencies NORAD does not have access to other agencies and their current activities. So, it is quite possible that NORAD had no idea what was happening in the area. During the actual operation and after, it would not have been possible to ascertain what has happening in the area without specialized signal detection equipment. NORAD happened to pick up the signals and their instruments misinterpreted them as "thermal."

8. Is there some distinct electronic method of detecting an ET underground base? How does this method work?

Assuming that ETs work in an ultraviolet light source (as reported from contact stories) it might be possible to look for radio emissions that signal the generation of such light sources in areas where ET bases are suspected. (I have also read of human UFO research groups using ultrasonics to look for "cavities," metal-lined and natural, under the surface where underground bases are thought to be located.)

Remote Viewing or remote viewing?

The use of the term, remote viewing, other than in its strict scientific definition, has caused some concern for researchers. Particularly, using RV to investigate off-world enigmas has caused great distress to orthodox remote viewers. The very fact that viewers cannot get feedback on anomalous targets excludes them from being termed remote viewing at all. Joe McMoneagle, a former SRI remote viewer, has stated that the term can only be applied when the phenomenon is experienced under pre-set and strict laboratory conditions. Any other form of remote viewing can best be termed, he says, as a psychic experience or clairvoyance.

Swann has added his concern and he has documented how the term remote viewing was originally coined to identify a particular kind of experimental protocol, rather than a particular kind of psi ability. In particular, the concept of feedback is crucial to the definition of remote viewing. According to Swann, the remote viewing model consists of five definite components: a subject; active ESP abilities; a distant target; the subject's recorded responses; and confirmatory positive feedback. When one of these component parts is missing, remote viewing has not taken place. However, the world appears to have claimed remote viewing as its own, and it now appears to have two definitions: remote viewing as experimental protocol, and remote viewing as a generalized human cognitive ability.

Remote Applications

Regardless of what you call it, remote viewing does have many potential, practical applications. In the future, remote viewing could be used to locate astronauts lost in space, to seek out lost or nonfunctioning satellites, and report on space emergencies. Remote viewers could work alongside engineers, computer personnel, and medics to add a new dimension to emergency location work.

The mind is able to go where machines or the physical body cannot go. An adept viewer could enter a hostile environment, encountering flood, fire, chemicals, or other substances. A remote viewer could go out into space, into the hub of a nuclear reactor after a melt-down; the possibilities are endless.

Such a resource would be invaluable to industry. Psi engineers could be trained in the conventional sciences to enable them to report and describe potentially dangerous or threatening conditions. They would be non-risk trouble-shooters and their potential would be unlimited.

References

Bigelow Holding Company. 1992. *Unusual personal experiences: An analysis of the data from three national surveys.* Conducted by the Roper Organization.

McMoneagle, J. 1993. *Mind Trek.* Charlottesville, Virginia: Hampton Roads Publishing.

Ring, K. 1984. *Heading towards omega.* New York: William Morrow.

Swann, I. 1993. *Everybody's guide to natural ESP.* Los Angeles: Tarcher.

CHAPTER THREE

LOOKING BACK

Instant Karmic Replays

Following explorations into outer space, I decided to start looking at the space within and to ask if there were a way that we can remotely view our past, or even our own future? Millions of people believe in reincarnation. For many religions reincarnation is one of the tenets of their faith and there are many books available on the evidence that has been put forward for reincarnation. Some of the facts they have put forward has been convincing, such as documentary evidence of children who reveal knowledge of having been someone else in a previous life. Professor Ian Stevenson, a psychiatrist who teaches at the University of Virginia, has studied many of these children. They name people and places in distant locations that they knew in a prior life. When these are checked out they are usually correct. And why, when we dream, do we meet people and visit places that we recognize, yet have never met these people or visited these places in our present lifetime?

I used to believe that as we go from babyhood, through childhood, into adulthood and old age in our present life, we also progress through continuing life-times. I wondered how many lifetimes we had to travel through and what happened when we come to the last lifetime? My current theory is that we may have access to information from previous lifetimes. However, they may not be our lifetimes, but, for whatever reason, they fit the purpose. Another intriguing theory is that we live concurrent lifetimes. When we access information about another lifetime we may travel across time and space rather than back.

I have become increasingly convinced of the possibility of reincarnation and that we are, possibly, a composite of many past lives. Using remote viewing I have been able look back at the past and I have been both surprised and humbled by my perceptions.

Recovery through Reliving

Recently I came across the work of psychiatrist Brian Weiss and his first book *Many Lives, Many Masters* in which he documents his discovery that emotional problems in this life may have their root cause before we are even born. He proposes that by reliving past lives, patients can become aware of events that triggered ongoing mental and physical problems in this lifetime. Initially a conventional psychiatrist with an orthodox training, he encountered a patient, whom he names Christine in his book, who seemed to resist traditional healing techniques. Under hypnosis he asked her to go back to the time when her problems began. He expected her to relate some event from her childhood, instead she began to relate events from a seemingly past life which had direct relevance to her present condition. Even more amazing, she began to recover.

Since then Weiss has worked with many more patients using this unconventional mode of therapy. He also discovered that several of his colleagues, although seemingly conventional, harbored many unconventional theories relating to metaphysical issues.

This Mortal Coil

Exploring past lives through remote viewing has been an ongoing process of discovery. I feel like an archeologist, uncovering the sands of time to reveal the secrets hidden beneath. At each stage of uncovering a new part of my past lives I have attempted to find documented evidence of that time period. However, as my past lives have been fairly ordinary I have not had a great deal of success, although the search has been an exciting journey.

I did not discover my past lives in chronological order but have presented them that way. My first remembered "incarnation" was very humbling. I cannot put a historic date on the time period but it must have been very early in history. I was very primitive, male, and lived, possibly, in Africa. I did not have language but communicated very much through instinct and feeling.

Spiritual Explorations

People, in general, tend to categorize OBEs as either good or bad. Some born-again Christians teach that OBEs are the "work of the Devil." Whereas some "New Agers" imbue OBEs with perceptions of love and light and get very discouraged when they experience negative events. I believe neither is correct. As OBEs are part of our normal cognitive repertoire of behavior, we should expect to experience all aspects of life. And, if you choose to mentally travel in other dimensions, don't be surprised to perceive other dimensional events.

I would not call myself a religious person, although I am spiritual. I do believe in a cosmic creator but do not see him, or her, as an aged person in the heavens meting out parental justice. My parents, perhaps wanting to be on the safe side, had me confirmed, as an infant, in the Baptist tradition, and also had me christened in the Episcopalian Church, complete with Godparents. I was raised Baptist, started attending Sunday School at the age of two, and became a Sunday School Teacher at the age of sixteen. Most of my religious experience has been in the Baptist Church, with a brief forays into Pentecostalism, Buddhism, and Celtic traditions.

I became very discouraged with organized religion in my early twenties. I had met my first husband, and we wanted to be married in my Baptist home church in Wimborne, Dorset. Because he was divorced and older than me, the church elders held a meeting, to which I was not invited, and they decided that not only would the pastor not marry us, but that I should be "disciplined." What this meant, I never found out. As soon as I learned of the meeting I left the church. As it turned out, my husband was not a good choice for me, but I was angered by the church's punitive attitude, where there should have been love and guidance.

After twelve years with minimal church contact, I met and married my second husband. Again, it was not a good match but I was dismayed by the church's attitude. Impoverished, abused, and homeless a few months after the wedding, I was criticized by the church fathers for dividing the church in their sympathy for me. I just wanted to get on with my life and decided to follow my own spiritual path.

I think of myself as a neopagan, not a Pagan in the conventional manner, as I do not celebrate rituals or attend rites. I have returned, full circle, to the beliefs that I held in my childhood, outside of the church. I worship the changing seasons; the rebirth of all living things in the Spring; the downright fecundity of summer; the fruits of the fall season; and the cold beauty of winter. As a child, I had my own garden and I loved to dig my fingers into the rich, dark earth. I wrote poems in praise of Mother Earth and treasured her riches.

I no longer have a fear of death: I believe that when we die we go on to experience the next great adventure. However, I hope to live, in this lifetime, until I am an old, old woman and have earned every wrinkle and grey hair. When I was a little girl, I thought that by the time I was twenty-four years old, I would have done everything: married, had children, grown old. What else was left after twenty-four? When I reached that age, I realized that I hadn't even begun to experience all that Life had to offer.

Of Ghosts and Goblins

I grew up in a haunted house. Our home was a red brick, semi-detached house, built between the World Wars. We had a living room and kitchen downstairs; three small bedrooms and a bathroom upstairs. The only toilet was outside. There was a coal fire in the living room and we used kerosene heaters when we wanted to warm other parts of the house. We heated bath water from a gas boiler located above the bathtub. Compared to some families who were living in decrepit Victorian row homes, or even in prefabricated concrete homes, we felt we were lucky.

We heard the ghost, rather than saw it. Alan and I would be playing upstairs in our bedrooms. Suddenly, we would hear the springs on our parents' bed start squeaking and the wardrobe door would slam open, against the wall. There was no human person in the room at the time. We also heard footsteps coming up the wooden staircase but no visible person came to the top. We were scared and told Mum but she didn't believe us. We had heard that twin babies had died in the house before we moved in but we did not know the full story.

A few years ago, when I was visiting England, I took my niece, Alan's daughter, Joy, to see the house where her Dad and I grew up. The house looked much the same, except the apple trees in the back garden had been cut down.

As we stood in front of the house, the current resident came out to meet us. He shook our hands and said his name was George. We asked him about the ghost. His reply was astonishing. "Don't talk to me about the ghost," George said. He went on to tell us that when he and his family moved in, ten years earlier, his children started complaining about faces floating on the ceiling.

He and his wife disregarded the stories until his wife came home from work to see an apparition in the living room. Originally, the fireplace had a high mantleshelf, which had been replaced by a lower, modern tile one. The wife saw the figure of an old woman, with her elbow propped on, what would have been, the older, higher fireplace. She had a towel over one arm and she was looking into the corner of the room, to the right of the fire. The family started making inquiries and discovered from elderly folk in the village that the original family in the house had been a mother and her mentally ill son. The mother had cared for the son, who usually sat in the corner, depressed and sad. The son, eventually, killed himself.

It seemed as if the mother was still concerned and looking after him. George and his family, who were Catholic, called in the local priest to bless and exorcize the house and the disturbances ceased.

Most of my life I have had occasional glimpses of folk who are still lingering in this dimension. For example, there was "The Lady in Black." Between 1987 and 1992, I worked as Research Assistant at the Princeton Engineering Anomalies Research Laboratory in Princeton. Brenda Dunne was the laboratory manager and I rented the top floor of her house. Very often, she would give me a ride to the lab in the morning. One day, she stopped briefly in the shopping center to pick up her briefcase from the shoe repair store. Brenda went into the store and I stayed in the car, as it was only a brief stop.

Suddenly, around the corner of the building, came a woman on a black, old-fashioned, sit-up-and-beg type of bicycle. There was a wicker basket attached to the front, which contained a black leather purse. The woman was tall, over six foot, very thin, in her sixties (I guessed), with pure white, page-boy cut hair, bright blue eyes, and alabaster white skin. She was dressed in a black gabardine raincoat buttoned up to the chin and wore black laced-up shoes, like my grandmother used to wear.

The Woman in Black fell off her bike onto the ground. She sat there, with her back straight and her legs stuck straight out in front of her. Concerned, I got out of the car to help her. She looked at me with intense blue eyes and said something in a foreign accent which I did not understand. She gripped my hand, with an amazing strength, and I helped her get up. She placed her bicycle outside the shoe repair store and went in. I heard the bell jangle and through the plate glass window I saw her wander around the small, one-room store. I was concerned that she had left her purse in the bike basket. Eventually, the Woman in Black came out, got on her bike, and pedaled off erratically, across the parking lot.

Brenda then came out of the store, and, even though the lady had been in the store a good five minutes with her, Brenda said she had not seen her. We concluded that the Lady in Black was not from this world.

When an individual is open to certain dimensions, he is open to many different types of experiences: positive and negative. I have experienced the good guys and the bad, the beautiful and the ugly; ghosts, goblins, and ghouls, from many different dimensions. Currently, I work in the here-and-now dimension, but occasionally other energies intrude, which need stronger measures to send them where they ought to be.

In 1993 I was invited to take part in a "ghost-busting" in Birmingham, Alabama. A team of psychics was called to investigate a range of anomalous events that were happening to two young veterinarian students. In their small apartment they experienced strange sounds, smells, voices, furniture moving, knocks and raps. They had tried to clear the intrusions themselves with a White Light ritual and attempted to contact the spirits with a Ouija board. The intrusions got worse, not better.

The ghost-busters decided to use a table-tilting technique to communicate with the deceased family that they felt were causing the disturbances. I was asked to sit in and I did—wearing my hat of the skeptical scientist. I wanted to watch the table, in particular where people put their hands and if they lifted or moved the table. They used an old, wooden-topped Victorian card table with metal legs. I wanted to see which side of the table went up and who was lifting it.

We sat around the table in candlelight, and at first nothing happened. Small scratches and raps could be heard under the table. Then the table started vibrating. I could clearly see everybody's hands on the table top and the table appeared to be moving independently under their hands. It was too late to back out. It was like being on a roller coaster, once it starts you are on for the ride. The table vibrated some more and then went up in the air—on my side.

Over the next few hours, the table responded to "yes" and "no" questions by raising up on two, and sometimes three legs. We deduced that the family had consisted of a mean man who had a very subservient wife and a small daughter. The husband had killed the wife and daughter, and then himself. At one point, one of the psychics stopped and said, "We have a problem; how do we let them know they are D-E-A-D?" The group decided to direct the family to the "light" and the movements of the table ceased. We were exhausted. It was reported to us a few weeks later that the disturbances had stopped.

Coping with Negative or Unwanted Intrusions

OBEs have been a good part of my life since I was a little girl growing up in Bristol. Most of my OBEs have been positive, but occasionally there have been events which have scared and confused me. There have been "black clouds" that hovered over my physical body. These were upsetting and I wondered if they were a portent of my own death. After a few of these, I realized they were linked with deaths within my family, mostly uncles.

Not all intrusions are negative. For a while, in Princeton, there was a little "voice" of someone or something that was learning about beauty and human reactions to ecstasy. After a few weeks, when it had satisfied its curiosity about human nature, it went away. However, not all intrusions are as benign as this one.

However careful you are, shielding yourself in white light or protecting yourself with good vibes, stronger, negative energies can sometimes intrude. What do you do about them?

Individuals who purposefully direct their remote perception to view historic or notable events, like a battle or natural disaster, may experience the horror and terror of the event. Many people who learn to direct their remote perceptions think that they will see the event, as if on television or as a movie. What often happens is that they experience what Lyn Buchanan calls Perfect Site Integration (Ingo Swann refers to it as Bilocation). The perceiver feels he is actually at the site: seeing, hearing, touching, tasting and smelling everything, as well as feeling all the emotions associated with the target. This can be overwhelming to some viewers. If you are one of these individuals, you can either choose not to perceive emotionally-laden sites, or you can remind yourself, during a stressful viewing, that you are just an observer, that the events have already happened. Be aware that if you choose to perceive alternative dimensions, you might perceive events, people, and places that could be disturbing to your earth-bound psyche.

What happens when another, living person's energy intrudes on your personal mind space? This can happen during the waking or sleep states. For instance, last year, as I was falling asleep, I sensed an acquaintance in my awareness, saying inappropriate things. What I have found most effective is to visualize a "mental mirror." When I felt the intrusion I would turn the "mirror" towards the intrusion, reflect back the intrusion to its source and it would cease. This might be just a psychological ploy, but it works.

I think of myself as a mentally healthy person; others see me as a very stable individual. However, a few years ago I experienced a negative intrusion into my waking life that really shook me up. I was working part-time in an office building in Las Vegas that housed several therapists' offices. One day I sensed an energy that was not mine. It was spiteful, male, angry, destructive, and sadistic. It attached itself to me. For the forty-eight hours it was with me, it suggested ways to harm myself and others, using language that I would never use. I reasoned that I must have picked up "something" from the building. Each time it suggested something harmful, I would say in a firm mental voice "No," hoping it would get bored and go away on its own. Eventually, I had enough of this interruption and did a purposeful meditation where I voiced aloud, "Go away. I do not want you in my head, in my body, in this house, in this family, in this place. Go away." It went away and never came back.

I have also discovered that there is a way to shield yourself from unwanted physical intrusions. When I first came to the States, I was living in a high-crime area. My first job was about two miles from my home. Being recently divorced and penniless, I did not have a car, and buses did not go to that part of town. So I walked every day, to and from work. However, I was constantly aware that I could be mugged or attacked—several other women had been attacked in the area. So, I devised a mantra that I repeated, silently, to myself to convey that all I carried in my bag were "books and shoes, books and shoes." Which was usually all I had anyway. Then, one day, I decided to challenge this belief. I changed the mental mantra to "lots of money, thousands of dollars, lots of money. " Near my home I was stopped by two young thugs, who wouldn't let me pass. I immediately changed the silent mantra to "books and shoes, books and shoes" and they walked on past me. I was amazed and thankful.

The Christos Experience

I first came across the Christos Experience during the metaphysical classes at Manchester University in England. I learned that through a process of complete bodily relaxation and suggestion a subject could be enabled to access the life history of another person. Several books have been written on the subject including *Windows of the Mind* by G.M. Glaskin. The Christos Experience sounded like an interesting phenomenon to try and so, during a class, several of the students went through the procedure. Some relived parts of their earlier present lives, whilst others seemed to talk about lives which were definitely not their own, either in character or time-period. Peter related part of his childhood in rural Canada, while Gwenn remembered part of a life as a South American Indian woman, maybe Aztec or Tolmec. Each student recounted a different experience. Of course, none of the experiences were verifiable, and were seen, by the majority, as an interesting mental exercise.

Iron Age Avon

During early December 1978 I decided to see if I could use the Christos Experience, in a modified way, to achieve a past-life regression. I tried to project not only to another place but another time-period. During one of these experiences I visualized a scene from Iron Age England. At this point I am not certain whether this occasion was just an experience that transcended the time barrier or whether this was a true memory of a previous life.

The location that I viewed was an iron age settlement at Seamills, a location on the outskirts of my home town, Bristol, in Avon, England.

I arrived at a small waterfall about 15 feet high which fell into a shallow pool a couple of yards across. The pool was surrounded by grass banks, trees and ferns. The waterfall fell down a cliff of rock. A man was bathing in the pool, under the waterfall. He did not have any clothes on, had very straight fair hair and light skin. He was young, lean but not very tall, perhaps just over five feet tall. I was watching him from a point to his left. The pool ran into a stream which then ran downhill to a valley where there was a river. The air was warm—summertime.

I watched the boy bathing for a while, then he was joined by a woman who looked like him. They both washed, then left by the right hand side of the waterfall. I watched for a while longer and saw a boy child of about two years old come down to the water in the pool. He was picking up leaves and sticks, throwing them in the water, and watching them float away down the stream. He was totally absorbed in his game. He did not see his mother come up behind him. She stood there, maternal, proud, watching her baby with a smile on her face. He was still entranced in his game. Then he began to follow the leaves and sticks down the stream. His mother walked in front of him, picked him up and carried him, screaming, around the right hand side of the waterfall. I stayed and watched for a while longer but nothing else happened. So, I decided to cross over the pool and follow the path that I had seen.

I put my hand under the waterfall and it was cold. So was the pool of water as I waded across. The bottom of the pool was rocks and boulders. Small fish swam in the pool and ferns grew around it. I climbed onto a grass bank and, to my surprise, there was a rough path going up through the trees. I had expected to see a village around the corner. Instead I climbed the path, up through the woods until I came out onto a grassy plain. I suddenly knew where I was. It was the high stretch of land between the Iron Bridge and Dingle Dell at Seamills, near my home village of Shirehampton, Bristol, in England, where I grew up in this lifetime. This high ridge of land, called Kings Weston, overlooks the River Avon on one side and the Severn Channel between England and Wales on the other side.

In the distance I could see smoke rising and hear dogs barking. I walked up to a circular settlement. It was surrounded by upright tree-trunks, very close together, with pointed tops. There was a space at the entrance. I looked quickly inside but I was scared that someone might see me. I saw neat thatched huts. There were people and dogs walking around. Two women were talking, with babies on their hips. Nobody had any clothes on, which surprised me (modern England is notoriously stormy and generally chilly, even in summertime). At this time, I was finding it hard to concentrate on the image, so I ended the session.

Searching for Confirmation

In March of 1979 I called my aunt Marge, who was a local historian, and had lived all her life in Shirehampton. I learned from her about an Iron Age barrow settlement that is up on Kings Weston. There were other Iron Age remains around the area. My father also confirmed that there were Iron Age fortifications up on Kings Weston Hill, but I did not know this before the session. I can remember playing in the grassy mounds up there when I was a child but did not know what they were.

In July, I visited the Bristol City Museum where they had a new exhibition of local historical sites. Here, I found some interesting information. It seems that during the period that I saw, the weather was a lot warmer than it is now and that there was a large Iron Age settlement up by Dingle Dell on the hill, as well as another one farther along at Blaise Castle. I also wrote to the University Museum for more information. By August I received information from the Assistant Curator in Archeology and History from the City of Bristol Museum. In their letter I found further details of the historical remains that are on top of Kings Weston Hill. On top of the hill was a fort, surrounded by a rampart, a ditch, and a counter-scarp bank. This was excavated at some time.

The letter further stated, "moving westward along the top of the hill (towards the quarry) is encountered the low remains of a circular enclosure. Then in the middle of the ridge is the remains of another rampart crossing the hill with a ditch on its west side. Excavations of the circular enclosure had produced pottery. Near the quarry were five barrows (burial chambers) which had been excavated and had produced pottery of the Late Bronze-Early Iron Age tradition. Down at the west side was another, barely visible round enclosure." The report from the museum added that during times of unrest, people would live within the confines of the enclosures for security, but normal life would take place in the good farmland that surrounded the Hill.

Time Transportation

Later in the year, my friend Peter and I took a walk up to the area where I had perceived the Iron Age settlement to be. Here we experienced some strange events, which included a distortion of time and space, anomalous light and sounds, and changes in temperature. Some would call it a time portal. It was a bitterly cold day in December, even though the sun was shining. I wanted to show Peter the hill and we sat up on top of the fortification. I was overcome with sleepiness and felt very warm. I took off my coat and lay down on the grassy mount. Peter, play-acting, began intoning a funeral dirge. I perceived an intense blue light which was so bright that I had to squeeze my eyes shut. When I opened them the sky was still the iron grey it had been when we climbed the hill. We heard strange sounds like a small animal being killed and crackling sounds like a fire, but there was no smoke to be seen. When we came down off the mount we found it bitterly cold again and had to put our coats back on. Did we shift back in time to an earlier era?

Viewing Your Own Grandmother

When I was working at Princeton University there were many opportunities to interact with metaphysical groups. The local Unitarian Church sponsored a women's spirituality group and here I found myself welcomed and accepted. During a guided meditation at one of these sessions I was able to access my English heritage and literally discovered my "roots."

The theme of the evening session was "discover your ancestors" and, through a type of visual imagery, we walked a path and found a tree. I visualized myself walking through Penpole Woods, a popular nature spot near my childhood home. It was autumn and misty and there was a smell of old leaves. I found the fairy circle, a group of tall beech trees that were growing in a circle. There is local lore that this circle was once used by Druids in their ceremonies. The tallest beech used to look so tall to me as a child, it seemed to touch the sky and I had to lean back to see the top.

During the meditation I saw the roots of this tree as old and gnarled and deeply embedded in the rock and soil, like our family, which has had connections with the area for about 500 years. In the session we were instructed to ask the tree a question and to go into the roots. I wanted to ask about finding a half-brother who lived somewhere in Germany. During the Second World War my father was a prisoner-of-war in Poland, and he fell in love with a Russian woman, who was also a prisoner. She had a child, fathered by my dad. After the war ended she married a German and moved to Germany.

When I asked the roots about my half-brother, I got the reply that "it is not important for the roots to always meet; by growing off in different directions the roots can stabilize and nourish the family tree." I had always hoped to find my half-brother, but perhaps it was not so important.

I thought that the meditation had finished and came out of the tree to find the woods of my imagination filled with all the children connected to our family tree. They were playing in the woods and dressed in period costume. They were running, jumping, calling out to each other, and climbing trees. I recognized a family resemblance among the children's faces. Then I saw my grandmother, Nana Win, as a young girl of about sixteen, at a family picnic.

She looked like my cousin Gwen as a young woman. I called her and said, "Nana Win, is that you?" She replied, "No, I'm Win, that's Nan," and pointed to her sister Ann (whose nickname was Nan).

Nana Win and I talked and I told her about her children, grandchildren, and great-grandchildren. She asked me "Who will I marry?" and I told her "Richard Powell." She was ecstatic. I saw her go to him and say she knew that they were going to marry. He replied, "But I haven't asked you yet."

From this meditation I realized that our family tree not only stretches a long way back in history but has its roots deeply entrenched in the rock and soil of Bristol. The roots are old and gnarled but very strong. I feel honored that I have inherited certain qualities that have been carried on down the centuries, certain facial characteristics and traits that have continued for centuries and generations. There is a certain myth that involves meeting your own grandparents and somehow altering the course of history. I don't believe that remote viewing of the past affects anything tangible.

Burned as a Witch

Several dreams sparked my quest to uncover a possible fourth previous life. One in particular intrigued me as it would provide an answer to certain fears I had including a fear of fire. However, whenever I attempted to uncover this particular life, I kept coming up against mental blocks. The dreams involved a farmhouse set in a rural part of England and I felt that I was connected in some way to that place. But the feeling that something awful had happened was too strong to let me perceive that time and place for any length of time. In August 1982 I finally overcame the block and unraveled the knot. What I discovered was the life of a farm girl who was gifted in healing animals. However, her behavior marked her as a witch and she was burned by her neighbors. This experience answered an important question for me. As a little girl I was terribly afraid of fire. Now I knew why.

The King's Mistress

In the April of 1979, I had another dream which indicated memories of a possible, past lifetime. It was of a house and a woman who I have dreamed of many times during the last twenty or so years. The house was situated in a wood or forest, was single-storied, and was probably a lodge-house. The woman who lived there was called Mary Cawley. I feel that I may have been Mary Cawley (pronounced Cowley). The dream I had in April 1979 was of the house in modern times, and it had been turned into a museum. However, I knew that the house had not been preserved as I knew it. I seemed to know what it was like as it was known by the woman called Mary Cawley. In the same dream I saw myself as an old woman, lying in bed, dying, in the end room of the house. The room was dark and dirty. The next room was full of books. It was a very old house.

The next morning, after the dream, I felt that I knew the story of the house; that it was a king's hunting lodge, between the 1600s and the 1700s. Mary Cawley was the king's mistress who lived at the lodge, and he came to visit her (me) there. We used to sit and read his books together. As we both aged he visited me less and less, and he left me the lodge when he died. I grew old there, read a lot, and died alone.

How do I know so much about this woman, Mary Cawley? How do I know so much about her life, her love, and her death? I see the house so clearly in my mind; I am so familiar with it but it is so frustrating not to know where it is so that I can visit it again.

During previous dream visits the house has been the same, a low, brick/stone building, but each dream has been during a different time in its history. On one occasion I recall entering the front hall and going into a small room to the left of the house. At another time, I dreamed that I arrived at the house to find it locked and neglected, the windows wired over. I looked through the dirty windows to gaze at the rooms, all empty except the end room, which was full of boxes, as if things were in storage.

Following the Trail of the Herb Strewer

From April until October 1979, I thought no more about the house or had any more dreams. Then my friend Gwen lent me a book, *A Book of Aromatics* by Roy Genders. I didn't get round to reading it until January of 1980 and, when I did, I found another possible link to the life of Mary Cawley. I read the following: "the strewing of aromatic herbs played an important part on ceremonial occasions. For example, at the time of the accession of James II, one Mary Cowle, was strewer of herbs in ordinary to His Majesty."

Could this be the same Mary Cawley but with her name spelled differently, as was common in early England? This was a far-flung coincidence. The dates seemed to coincide. James II acceded in 1685, but was only king for three years, and Mary Cawley, as I knew her from my dreams, had a knowledge of plants and herbs that would qualify her as a "strewer of herbs."

But, when I consulted *A History of England* I found that James II was a different type of personality to the king that I had known when I was Mary Cawley. Who preceded James II? It was Charles II.

I was reading through a book, *History of Bristol's Suburbs*, in February 1993 when I found more interesting information. I bought the book in January 1981 before coming to live in the States and it had come with me and all my books to my adopted country. In Chapter 16, entitled "Abbots's Leigh," I found that Charles II had stayed close to Bristol in 1651.

I went back to Feiling's *A History of England* to find that Charles II became King of England in 1660 when he was thirty years of age and died in 1685 when he was only 55 years of age. The year 1651 saw the fall of Worcester and Charles's flight south. His stay at Abbot's Leigh occurred during October 1651. He was sheltered by Royalists and Catholics in his epic flight from Boscobel to Sussex, and in October found a ship at Brighton which carried him to France. Charles died of a stroke on February 6, 1685, and he received the last rites of the Catholic Church from Father Huddleston (who also helped him in his escape from Worcester).

Abbot's Leigh is about one mile from where my paternal great-grandmother's family lived at Easton-in-Gordano. Of all my grandparents and great-grandparents, I feel that she is the one that I most favor in terms of personality and intelligence. She was a Porter by birth and Porters have lived in this area for many hundreds of years.

I grew up in the village of Shirehampton, about one mile from Abbot's Leigh, and Shirehampton has some quaint old customs that connect it to Abbot's Leigh. A further historical note links Abbott's Leigh to other religious activities: it was a monastic retreat for many centuries, and it had mystical connections. Thomas Norton (the Nortons were the owners of Abbot's Leigh for many years) figured largely in the fifteenth century by claiming to have discovered the Philosopher's Stone and the Elixir of Life.

Another interesting piece of information that confirmed that Charles II, even in later life, was still visiting the Shirehampton area comes from our local church, St. Mary's in Shirehampton. This information also links our family, the Porters, again with Charles II. In an old prayer book, formerly used in the old Shirehampton chapel and now kept in the church, is the following inscription on the fly-leaf:

> *Mr. Thomas Alcock, chosen arbitrator by both parties to end a controversie did award Richard Brittaine, a Quaker, to pay for this common prayer book and surplice for the use in Shierehampton Chapel, because he assaulted William Porter, one of the King's boatmen, February, 1682.*

When I attended Portway Secondary School in Shirehampton, two of my girl friends were Brittaines and their family religion was still Quaker. The information about the prayer-book was discovered when I wrote to my Aunty Marge in Shirehampton, asking her for information about our family history. This was in the spring and the summer of 1983. I had never heard any of this family history prior to that date but found it fascinating. It gave me a good feeling of belonging to Shirehampton and the surrounding area, and of having well-established roots in English soil.

However, it could be that the Mary Cawley experience is not, after all, a past life remembrance, but an example of cryptomnesia—a buried memory from our current lifetime which is sometimes invoked to explain an apparent paranormal awareness. An example of cryptomnesia would be someone hearing a foreign language as a very young child and then attributing that knowledge, during an altered state of consciousness, to a past life experience. Another theory is that we possess a "racial memory" whereby information is passed down at the cellular level from ancestor to descendant.

Another piece of information that fits the puzzle came to light in 1980 when I was living in Manchester. A cutting from a local newspaper bears the headline "Will Maria wed her guardsman." The cutting bears a photograph of a smiling young woman with dark eyes and hair. The text reads:

Left a widow at 28 when her husband Earl Cowley died tragically playing squash, Argentine-born Maria, Countess of Cowley has found new happiness with another bereaved person.....Cowley, who was descended from the brother of the Iron Duke of Wellington, died aged 20. His father Dennis, the fifth earl, also died of a heart attack in equally sporting circumstances - entertaining a lady of the night.

Critics would be quick to point out that, perhaps, my early dreams and visualizations were a precognitive knowledge of this newspaper article. That is one possible explanation but precognitive dreams usually occur within a very short time of the event occurring. My dreams of Mary Cawley had occurred over many years and had covered many different circumstances in her life.

The Rich, Bored Widow of Shropshire

I uncovered another possible past life, that of Miriam Banquet, in 1979 during the Christos experiments, and I decided to take another look at her life. Miriam was wealthy and lived in luxury in a big house in the north of England. I knew that she was born Miriam Levine, and she was married to Peter Raymond Banquet, a businessman. They had no children and she had always enjoyed a privileged lifestyle.

This had been one of my first Christos sessions and had resulted in the revelation of a very sad woman indeed. I felt very sorry for Miriam Banquet. Throughout the experience I was both her and me. I could feel the great heaviness of her unhappiness, yet at the same time I could objectively look around and take note of my surroundings.

Her misery became so oppressive that I didn't feel that I could stay with her any longer, and the session ended. I had the feeling that perhaps she would take her own life. In my present life I have never been as depressed as this woman was; but, having experienced her unhappiness, I have a new sympathy for people who are depressed. Her depression was like a heavy weight that nothing could shift—all her money and possessions meant nothing to her.

During the weekend of August 14, 1983, I decided to have another look at the life of Miriam Banquet. Previously, I thought that she came from Yorkshire, but in the following session found that she came from Shropshire in England. Miriam Banquet was born Miriam Levine at "Fairlawns." The family name is Jewish but her family was Roman Catholic. The second session took the form of an unusual mental dialogue between me and Miriam. This was not a "channeled dialogue" as such, but I felt as if I were both me and Miriam. I would ask questions and the voice of Miriam would answer but I had an insight into the answers as if I knew a lot of the details that Miriam disclosed.

The Short, Sad Life of Nicola Dubrec

Another life that I uncovered, in July 1992, was of a French girl called Nicola Dubrec, who lived in Paris during the 1940s. She lived with her Spanish mother and French father at an inn that they owned. Unfortunately, Nicola became alcoholic by the age of sixteen and died in a fall when she hit her head on a stone floor. For years I had been familiar with the name Nicola. When, as a child, I was asked what name I would like to have other than my own, I always answered Nicola. I thought that I would call a daughter Nicola. Later, I thought about using the name for a pen-name. I feel that Nicola Dubrec was my most recent remembered lifetime. It is sad that she only had sixteen years of life and that it ended so suddenly.

It is interesting that twice during the ten prior lives that I uncovered, I have been male. The rest of these lives I seem to have lived as a female. Both of my male incarnations occurred early on in my lives-cycle. The two occasions that I was male were as a primitive hill tribesman, and as a peasant boy in Anglo-Saxon England. Most of my past lives were spent in Europe, specifically in England, around the area of my present-life birthplace. Twice, I lived in Paris. The majority of my past selves led very ordinary lives. The nearest I got to fame was as one of the possible mistresses of Charles II. Consequently, the glimpses I have had of these past lives have been everyday and humdrum.

The Naughty Italian Nun

After finding ways to access past lives, I decided to work with a therapist friend who was able to hypnotize me. Under hypnosis I was able to relocate the past life of a woman who lived in fifteenth century England, and the cloistered life of a nun in Italy during the seventeenth century. This was no pious nun. She had been retained in the nunnery as a young girl because of her unladylike behavior and all during her novitiate she had retained a sense of humor and adventure. Her greatest fun was to spy on the townspeople from a high grille in the nunnery wall. The details revealed through hypnosis were just as clear and colorful as those gained through remote viewing and the Christos Experience, suggesting that similar mental processes were at work in all three experiences.

References

Feiling, K. 1972. *A history of England*, 535–550. UK: Book Club Associates.

Genders, R. *A book of aromatics*. Publisher and date unknown.

Glaskin, G.M. 1974. *Windows of the mind: The christos experience*. London: Wildwood.

Jones, F.C., and W.G. Chown. 1977. *History of Bristol's suburbs*. Chapter 16. "Abbot's Leigh." Bristol, England: Reece Winstone Publications.

Landsburg, A. 1977. *In search of strange phenomena*. London: Corgi.

Stevenson, I. 1974. *Twenty cases suggestive of reincarnation*. Charlottesville, Virginia: University Press of Virginia.

Weiss, B. 1992. *Many lives: many masters*. New York: Simon & Schuster.

CHAPTER FOUR

LOOKING FORWARD

Fixing the Ozone Hole

During the winter of 1991 I met with a scientific colleague who had been working with remote viewing groups to assess future technologies, especially those that could help remedy planetary problems. He asked if I would like to undertake an informal viewing project. He let me review confidential reports from other projects that he had commissioned from multiple viewers, particularly perceived events surrounding the Tunguska Explosion in Siberia in the 1800s. I was impressed at the degree of concordance between the viewers' perceptions of these events. I was eager to tackle his project to locate future technology which might remedy the ozone problem.

On November 20th I did the first of two remote viewings of potential future technology. I looked at the future (possibly 30 years ahead) to assess how society will attempt to cope with the depletion in the ozone layer. I first saw large circular tanks in the California hills. These tanks evolved into a complex of storage tanks and a processing plant for cleaning and storing polluted ozone from auto and industrial emissions. This "waste" had been pumped to the tanks from over and around a large city, possibly Los Angeles. Ozone pollution is produced as a by-product of auto and other pollution when it interacts with sunlight.

However, it is "dirty" and needs to be collected, measured, "scrubbed" of particles and measured again, before it can be released into the upper atmosphere. The ozone is "lofted" into the atmosphere by means of upward wind currents off of the sea, which produces some natural ozone of its own, and by a solar-assisted thermal venting process. Many large polluted cities could be candidates for this process. The "lofting" mechanism doesn't actually reach the upper atmosphere but assists the ozone high enough for it to rise of its own volition.

The next day I completed the second remote viewing to locate and identify technical devices to process ozone to supplement the depleted atmospheric levels. However, I felt that both of these technologies might be implemented too little and too late. Thermally-processed ozone, sufficiently heated by thermal ocean currents and solar energy, could be "lofted" up to supplement the depleted layers. I saw a processing unit which could float on the ocean, possibly constructed from a ceramic material, approximately thirty to fifty feet in diameter and covered with solar tiles. It glistened in the sunlight, aesthetic as well as functional. Descending into the ocean was a rigid pipe to collect filtered seawater. This, too, was between thirty to fifty feet in diameter to provide stability. The unit was not tethered but floated in the natural current, rather like a fisherman's float. Rising from the unit was a vent, also thirty to fifty feet tall to discharge the processed ozone. Inside the body of the unit was a catalytic process which created ozone from exposure to ocean thermal energy and solar energy. While these technologies might help clean up the atmosphere, will they be in time? Will such technologies come too late?

In April 1998, seven years after completing this project, I finally received feedback on the feasibility of these perceptions. Melvin L. Prueitt, a guest physicist at the Los

Alamos Laboratories in New Mexico, recently gave an interview to Douglas Page, a freelance writer for *Spirit*, the in-flight magazine for Southwest Airlines. Melvin Prueitt recently patented a method to rehabilitate smoggy air using 600-foot "air-scrubbing" towers. According to Prueitt, "100 such towers could wash half the air in smoggy cities such as Los Angeles or Mexico City every day." Prueitt envisions these towers to be aesthetic as well as functional. According to Page, the first towers of Prueitt's design could emerge within a year or two.

The 2030 Exodus

The following remote viewing, entitled "The Exodus," was initiated during a time of exploration, in February of 1987, when I wanted to find out whether I could remote view the future, as well as the past and present. What I viewed troubled me greatly and I realized that I had a responsibility to share this information. The Exodus commences in the year 2030 and covers a time period of about fifty years. In this scenario it appears that the Earth's atmosphere, particularly around the northern hemispheres, undergoes a rapid, unexpected, and devastating deterioration, necessitating the evacuation of the people of the north to the lands around the Mediterranean. Many die on the journey and assimilation into the new cultures is difficult. Eventually the northern atmosphere resolves and people start returning to their ancestral lands to begin a new life. I chose the name "Exodus" to denote the mass moving of entire nations under conditions of duress and distress.

I landed on a green grassy hill. All around me was lush vegetation, birds and a few rabbits. They did not appear to be threatened by my presence. Things seemed much the same. I looked for the Uffington white-horse carved into the hillside but sensed it was grassed over and neglected.

I decided to move to another location and looked for a way to do this. At the bottom of the old roadway I saw a plastic bubble about five feet wide, having a reclining seat in the middle. I did not see any controls. I used my mind to move the bubble, which I took to be transportation. I floated high over towns and villages and finally came down in the small town of Canterbury.

Strangely, all the houses and shops were closed and boarded up. Nothing looked damaged. There were plenty of birds around. I stood in a square in front of Canterbury Cathedral. Behind me was the town square where markets were held but the space was empty. In front of me stood the huge wooden doors of the cathedral. On the door was fastened a large printed notice. I tried to read it but I wasn't able to. I tried to decipher it mentally and discovered that it outlined plans for a massive evacuation of people. Inside the cathedral, it was calm and quiet. Light came through the stained-glass windows. There was dust and dirt on the floor and I saw at least two dogs walking around. I left the cathedral and traveled to London.

I arrived on the Thames Embankment, near Westminster. The river was flowing as usual and there were lots of pigeons around—but still no people. I also traveled to New York's Battery Park and Red Square in Moscow, but it was all the same. Everything looked okay, wildlife and domestic animals around—but people missing.

In March of the same year I made another attempt to view these events. I arrived in a forest and walked through on a footpath until I came to a clearing overlooking a small village or town. The town was boarded up and overgrown. People had not been around for some time. I then traveled to Canterbury, which was the next town. I found the same notice nailed to the Cathedral door but it was faded and torn by the elements. Evidently some time had passed since my last visit.

I went to where all the people were. I found myself in one of the countries surrounding the Mediterranean. I knew that this was where the bulk of the people had fled. Some wealthy people had bought some of the islands, such as Corfu and Majorca, and were living there in some style, trying to maintain some semblance of education, culture, and technology. However, in general, all the major systems of education, communications, long-distance air travel, and technology had broken down, as had the major political and religious groups.

The major cause of the Exodus was a dramatic escalation of the destruction of air quality. Society thought it had many more years to reverse the damage (even in 2030), but the whole atmosphere suddenly collapsed over the northern hemisphere. It was dramatic and unexpected. There were only a few weeks in which to move down to the Equatorial countries.

The "exiles," as they are called, live in kibbutz-type communities. Since their countries have been lost, people become very family- and people-oriented. Extended families live in single-story, extended houses with many rooms for all of the family members. The houses are white-washed and functional.

The main work is food related, either growing or preparing food. People who have never farmed or gardened are now learning. Many people have died through sickness related to tropical disease, malnutrition, and stress. The main concern is to get enough food to eat.

For entertainment, people get together in the evening to sing, act in plays, and read from books that have been salvaged, trying to keep a little culture in their lives. Some of the younger people date the local young people and marry. This is not generally approved of by the exile community who talk about an eventual return to their own countries.

Some false religions have sprung up, making grand promises and suggesting ways to return to their home countries. These men become quite powerful in their communities.

The host countries have been benevolent, have provided land, have promised seed and aid, but have not allowed the exiles to participate in the running of the countries. With the collapse of the north, the whole world economy has suffered.

Long-distance air travel is no longer feasible because of the air quality; only trips of an hour or less by plane are possible. There are also fuel shortages. There are some of the "bubble" cars in use that I saw on my last visit, but to my surprise, many people use bicycles to get around.

In terms of communication, there was a surge of satellite communication before the exile, which was available even to the average person. However, most of this system collapsed, as did the newspapers, radio, and television. Eventually, small groups began to produce local newspapers, especially on the islands, and some satellite communication still exists.

I managed to look a little further and saw that the atmospheric system does eventually heal and there is a gradual return to the home countries for the exiles. The "islanders," as they are called, come forward as the future leaders and there is a gradual re-integration and growth. Some of the exiles prefer to stay in the host countries, especially if they were born there or married locally. The return takes about 50 years and should begin about 2070.

The Big One in the Big Apple

By 1992 I had been working for about a year with Intuition Services, headed by Ryan Wood, which also solicited earthquake information, and ran a 900 service called Quakeline. Ryan was interested to see if I could predict the impact and timing of future Earth changes. The following remote viewing was specifically focused on future earthquakes that would cause major Earth changes. There has been speculation that "The Big One"—the next gigantic California quake—will separate most of the California coast, sending it into the Pacific Ocean. What I viewed, however, was an Earth-changing event which occurs on the East coast of America. As mentioned before, Ryan Wood would send me a list of questions related to the viewing that needed to be accomplished. These were my responses which pointed out that the next "Big One" could very well be in the "Big Apple."

Report to Intuition Services

The problem description from Intuition Services said the following: Data from several independent sources have predicted cataclysmic volcanic and earthquake activity to occur throughout the world. A specific sequence of events has been hypothesized leading up to the final sinking and re-arrangement of the west coast of America. Gather the remote viewing scenario for Earth changes and compare/contrast with existing data. The following questions were supplied by Intuition Services to which I responded with the following answers:

1. Specifically when and where will the next major quake occur with significant damage/drastic implications for the United States or the world?
The next major quake which will occur with significant damage/drastic implications for the United States and the world will be in the New York and New Jersey area, specifically affecting New York City/Manhattan, although other major cities and towns will suffer severe damage.

2. Describe in detail the geography of destruction (faults, hills, cities). How will water, power, pipelines, communications, and transportation be affected, both short and long term?

Manhattan lies in the path of a major fault that created the foothills of New Jersey. There is a fault that underlies central Manhattan that has been active in the past. Manhattan was once two islands but surface activity filled in the rift thousands of years before the arrival of the Europeans, who found it one island.

The destruction will be catastrophic and was difficult to view because of the viewer's feelings of horror at the extent of the damage, both to property and life. Loss of life in the subway system is particularly appalling. The quake occurs in the dark and it is cold, which hampers rescue efforts. The island is basically split in two across the middle, first affecting Chinatown and Little Italy. The quake pushes the two halves of the island apart laterally causing property damage up- and down-town. Water, power, pipelines, and transportation are all destroyed but some communication, which does not rely on power lines, will be maintained.

3. Describe the aftermath, fires, logistics problems, flooding or any other significant problems. What are the things or skills that are needed most to speed recovery and repair?

Prior to the quake, many puzzling small ground fires arise in the New Jersey and New York areas, which are later found to be due to natural gas leaking to the surface and spontaneously combusting. Looking out over Manhattan from the New Jersey foothills before the quake, a much heavier than usual haze lies over the city, making the lights shimmer.

The aftermath of the quake is terrible: many major fires, roads are torn up and twisted, and communication and power lines are torn apart as the island separates. The major change that occurs is that water from the rivers on either side of Manhattan flood into the central rift causing it to flood. This central waterway will eventually be named the Manhattan Strait (some will affectionately call it The Canal). The skills most needed to speed recovery and repair will be:

a. air-borne lighting (the waterways around the island will be too disturbed for waterway assistance),

b. air-borne water-delivery systems for the many fires (some will advocate letting the city burn),

c. medical and humanitarian aid to deal with the injuries and loss of habitation of millions of people,

d. political and public relations systems to defuse the public attitude that the city somehow deserved the catastrophe (this attitude could hinder financial and other aid to the city's recovery),

e. psychological assistance to enable the remaining residents to rebuild the city, taking advantage of the rift, the strait, and encouraging the rebuilding of communication, and building of bridges between the islands.

4. How will the average quake victims deal with the trauma? What are their fears, anxieties and hopes?

The average quake victim will be either dead or severely injured. The primary goal of the survivors will be to get medical aid, food, and shelter. Dealing with the trauma, their fears, anxieties, and hopes must wait until after their immediate survival needs are met. The devastation will be so great that, for a time, there will be a communal sense of total helplessness and apathy. Dealing with this aftermath will require a concerted and skilled effort from the rest of the nation.

5. Determine the timing of major/significant damaging quakes/Earth changes for the following cities: Tokyo, Southern California, San Francisco/Bay Area, Seattle, Missouri, New York and London, England.

Other major/significant damaging quakes/Earth changes will occur in Beijing, China; Denver, Colorado; the western coast of south and central America, specifically Santiago, Chile; and Mexico City, Mexico. Lesser quakes, in view of damage to persons and property, will occur in Alaska, the Ural mountains, and in Samoa. All these will occur within the next twenty years. I did not see any devastating damage occurring in other areas such as Tokyo, southern California, San Francisco/Bay Area, Seattle, Missouri, or London, England, although minor quake activity will continue.

6. Describe the sequence of geological events, what starts first, how do the changes progress significantly and what are the final series of quakes before a long, multi-year quiet.

Quakes will be preceded by anomalous events such as small ground fires, caused by the leakage and combustion of natural gas. Haze, before major quakes, will be characterized by its increasing density and its propensity to hug the ground, causing fogs. Water levels will fall, then rise dramatically. The quakes will increase in strength and proximity to each other in a westerly to easterly direction across the globe and will drift upward from the southern hemisphere to the north. The quakes will then lessen in intensity, followed by a long quake-free period.

7. Will any new large land masses be formed? If so, where and how big?

The only land masses that I saw formed were the two separate islands caused by the splitting of Manhattan.

8. Describe the implications/changes that result from volcanic eruptions? Which eruptions have the most impact on communities/countries both logically and globally.

I did not remotely-view any volcanic eruptions. I was focused on quake activity.

9. Are there any magnetic pole shifts in our short term fifty-year future? If so, describe direction, new poles, and impact on current and future society and commerce.

I did not detect any magnetic pole shift, although the fact that the quake activity shifted from the south to the north hemisphere could be a prelude to a later shift. I have no comments at this time on the impact of such a shift on current and future society and commerce.

While this viewing does not rule out a major quake on the west coast, it does point to a major impact on the east coast including devastating Earth changes. Following this viewing, I heard that several other remote viewers had also predicted the "Big One" in the "Big Apple." In addition, old maps were found from around 1933 that clearly showed three major fault-lines running centrally across Manhattan through the Bronx Park, Central Park, and lower Manhattan.

Following this viewing, details were sent to a representative of the United States Geological Survey in Albuquerque, New Mexico. He ridiculed the idea that a major quake, as described, would occur in the New York City area.

An interesting article appeared in the *New York Magazine* of December 1995, written by Fred Graver and Charlie Rubin, entitled "Earthquake: Not only can it happen here—but it will."

More than eighty people from different disciplines were interviewed for the article. The authors stated that although these individuals had "wildly competitive agendas" they all agreed on one thing: maybe not today, maybe not tomorrow, but a big quake is coming and New York is not ready for it. The authors also said that although the interviewees disagreed on how big, how devastating, and how soon it would come, nobody denied that New York was going to see a major earthquake.

What was most interesting to me in the article was an illustration showing Manhattan and detailing the 125th Street fault running horizontally right across Manhattan, at the north end of Central Park. The legend box detailed the fault lines that run through Manhattan saying:

> *Quake predictions center on the Newark Basin, which sits between the two 'belts' of fault that surround New York City. The first belt runs down from the Hudson Highlands. The second fans out through Winchester County, down through New York City, and into central New Jersey.*

Future Earth Changes

Projections of major Earth changes have been made, in recent years, by Gordon-Michael Scallion. Copies of his maps detailing the re-flooding of the Great Basin area in the southwestern United States have become very popular. During a workshop that I was giving on remote viewing in 1995 I looked at these changes to see if there was additional material to add to Scallion's predictions.

During a portion of the workshop, when we were meditating to a recording of shamanic drumming, the following information was perceived. I have called it the "White Crow Vision" because of the beautiful Native American dancer in white feathers who danced for me. She conveyed the story in dance as it was told to me by Native American drummers.

At first I was sitting facing a large fire. Drummers were sitting around the fire, drumming in rhythm to the recording. They asked if I had a question to ask. My response was that I would like to ask about the flooding of the southwestern United States that was predicted by Gordon-Michael Scallion. They laughed and said that, yes, it was going to happen. They then showed me how, over the centuries, the Great Basin area has cyclically filled and emptied. Sometimes the area is a great inland sea, at other times it is a desert. Visually, I perceived the whole southwestern half of the United States greening, filling with water, emptying and drying, then filling again over the centuries. However, the cycles took many thousands of years to complete. This was the natural order of things and would happen regardless of human activity.

Remote viewing is a mental tool that can be used to access information about present targets, to look at historic events, as well as to project future happenings. It functions irrespective of time and space. However, with both past and present remote viewing there is the possibility of almost immediate feedback to reinforce the viewer's perceptions. With future viewing this feedback has to wait until the actual events have occurred. Some purists have argued that this cannot be called true remote viewing. They argue that the concept of feedback is essential to the definition of remote viewing. According to my definition, whether one gets feedback or not, the act of viewing by itself is the only necessary component of remote viewing. It stands alone as a valid human experience.

CHAPTER FIVE

PARTICIPATION

The Psychophysical Research Laboratories (PRL)

My serious participation in psi research began in 1986. I was working, at the time, as a researcher with Professor Michael Lewis' Institute for Child Development at the University of Medicine and Dentistry of New Jersey (UMDNJ) in New Brunswick. I had been hired in 1985 to be part of a research team that was investigating the cognitive development of premature infants who had developed brain bleeding.

During this period I was active and excited by my work. Yet, I felt I was neglecting those metaphysical aspects of my life that had once been so important to me. In the spring of 1996, I read about the Psychophysical Research Laboratory (PRL), located near Princeton, and learned that they were looking for volunteer subjects to participate in their psi experiments. Most of the participants who participated at PRL were "first-timers," people who had never taken part in parapsychology experiments. I was intrigued and wrote to PRL, who responded with questionnaires, and reprints about their work.

Some of their previous research has shown that individuals who have prior meditation experience, who had previous psi experiences, and fell into the ENFP (extraverted, intuitive, feeling, and perceiving) MBTI personality rating, were more likely to do well in psi experiments, such as the Ganzfeld. I fell into several of these categories.

On my days off, vacation days, and holidays I would catch the local train from New Brunswick to Princeton Junction. The laboratory was situated in an affluent, modern business park, surrounded by trees and lawns. I was surprised at the amount of space they had and learned that PRL was funded by a grant from the McDonnell Foundation. John McDonnell, one of the founders of the aerospace firm of McDonnell-Douglas, had a long-time interest in metaphysics and established a fund to carry out anomalies research. Here, I met the Director of PRL, Chuck Honorton, and his researchers, Marta Quant and George Hansen, who taught me a lot about critical thinking in psi research.

My first contact with Chuck was a bit of a shock. Nobody had told me that he suffered from brittle-bone disease and, consequently, was very short and walked with a stick because of his multiple fractures. However, what he lacked in height, he made up for in personality. He has been acclaimed as the best in his field and his Ganzfeld research has been used as a benchmark for further studies by the Edinburgh parapsychologists, and by social psychologist Daryl Bem. Chuck's early death, from a heart attack, while he was studying for his Ph.D. at Edinburgh, was a great loss for the parapsychological community.

During the following year and a half I was able to participate in several Ganzfelds, as well as taking part in psychokinesis (PK) computer games. I had also made a decision that, when my research at UMDNJ was over, I wanted to attend Edinburgh University in Scotland to study for my Ph.D. in parapsychology. The Psychophysical Research Laboratory graciously made available their extensive library and a computer. When I was not taking part in experiments, I was in the library, voraciously reading everything I could on parapsychology.

The Mind-Science Foundation

Motivated by my participation at PRL, I made inquiries about other labs doing parapsychology research and was able to take part in remote psychokinesis experiments conducted by the Mind-Science Foundation in Texas. Every few weeks I would be sent a tape of musical tones which had been pre-recorded. These tones were based on a random process and there should have been no discernable pattern to them. What the subject was asked to do was to cast their mind back to the time that the tape was recorded and to try and impose some order on the random process, to create higher or lower tones, or longer or shorter sequences of tones. This was quite a challenge, and I enjoyed the tasks, although I never did very well.

Princeton Engineering Anomalies Research (PEAR) Laboratory

During the time that I was visiting PRL I was aware that the lab's time was coming to a close. The funding was drying up, and going to more conventional study centers. The PRL staff suggested, as I was still interested in psi research, that I should contact the Princeton Engineering Anomalies Research (PEAR) Laboratory at Princeton University, where I could continue to be involved.

In 1983, Professor Robert Jahn, Brenda Dunne, and Roger Nelson had published Precognitive Remote Perception, a technical report in which they evaluated 227 formal precognitive remote perception trials. The results of this impressive body of data indicated that their efforts were highly significant. The PEAR document concluded that "precognitive remote perception techniques can acquire significant amounts of compounded information about spatially and temporarily remote target locations, by means currently inexplicable by known physical mechanisms."

My first visit to PEAR almost did not occur. I had no problem following directions I had been given to the lab, which is located in the School of Engineering and Applied Science of Princeton University, until I got to the basement and took a wrong turn. It seemed the lab kept such a low profile that even the students did not know that PEAR existed or even where it was located. Finally, I found the narrow orange door, simply labeled C131, that led to the lab. This label is deceptively simple; it gives you no indication of the wonders inside.

Visitors to the lab, particularly from overseas or from conventional laboratories, often ask "Where is the lab?" when they are standing right in the middle of it. Apart from the six computers, and arrays of other technology, the lab could be someone's home, complete with carpeting and sectional orange couch. However, it is not every home that can boast a ten foot tall pinball machine, used to test macro-psychokinesis. Other attractive, but very seriously scientific devices, are a pendulum, complete with crystal ball, and a water fountain bathed in colored lights.

After a few months' participation at PEAR, the project at the Institute for Child Development came to a close, and I had to decide what I wanted to do. Brenda Dunne approached me with an offer to work at the lab and I jumped at the chance. Brenda warned me that this would not be regarded by the scientific community as a good career move but what I was not prepared for was the scalding criticism that was poured upon me by my scientific colleagues. Scientists, whom I had admired for their openness and capacity for fairness, publicly berated me for daring to move to such a suspect area of research. Where was their commitment to freedom of inquiry? Being raised British and determined (some call it stubborn), I decided to put aside my plans for Edinburgh and make the move to Princeton. I am glad that I did.

From January 1987 to the Fall of 1992 my life became a kaleidoscopic inside view of the parapsychology field. The world and her brother came through the narrow orange door marked C131, into the often-bizarre world of the PEAR Lab.

PEAR was, originally, the conception of rocket scientist Robert Jahn, Professor Emeritus and past Dean of the School of Engineering—a respected, classical Princeton scientist. Fifteen years ago, one of his students approached him to ask if he would be her instructor for her under-graduate thesis. The topic she had picked, however, was highly controversial. She wanted to build a microelectronic random-number-generator (RNG) and replicate some of the psychokinesis experiments that had been carried out by Helmut Schmidt at the Mind-Science Foundation in Texas.

Jahn's immediate response was to discourage her but she reminded him of his commitment to free inquiry. He conceded on the terms that they would conduct site visits to the various parapsychological research laboratories and she would prepare a report to convince him of the need for such a project. They did this and, a year later, the student had completed her project and succeeded in obtaining significant results.

Jahn had kept his personal beliefs quite separate from his scientific research and teaching but he realized that if there could indeed be a subtle connection between the human mind and a device, like an RNG, then this was something that should be examined. We have entered an increasingly technical world, where even the slightest perturbation of an electrical signal can cause significant deviation from the normal operation of a device. If the device was a control system for a rocket, that slight deviation could have devastating consequences. So the PEAR Laboratory was born.

The lab's first experiment included another replication of the RNG experiment and Jahn brought on board Brenda Dunne, who had been investigating remote viewing experiments at the University of Chicago, and Roger Nelson, an experimental psychologist. Later, he added John Bradish, an engineer, and York Dobyns, a theoretical physicist, to complement the interdisciplinary team.

Brenda had conducted successful remote viewing experiments with Bisaha at Chicago University and met Jahn when she was giving a presentation of her work at a Parapsychological Association (PA) annual meeting. Setting up the lab was not easy, however, and Jahn and Dunne met a great deal of initial skepticism and resistance from the University authorities. Jahn, who had reached the top of his field in aerospace engineering, now became suspect for even daring to *think* about such topics as psychokinesis and remote perception, let alone set up a lab to study these topics.

In his capacity as Dean of the School of Engineering, Jahn was able to remodel part of the School's basement area into a laboratory, and, with the help of a private grant, furnished it, and added the equipment needed to set up the first experiments. The walls were paneled, the floor was carpeted, and the famous orange couch was installed. Later, he was successful in winning grant monies from several major funders, including the McDonnell Foundation and the Fetzer Foundation.

Jahn and Dunne complement each other perfectly. He is the hard scientist; the logical, sequential thinker; the fund-raiser; the front person with the credentials. Dunne is more "right brain," takes a more holistic approach, and is creative, spontaneous, imaginative, mystical, and intuitive. However, they both hide a side to their personalities that few people see. Jahn has a great sense of humor, a passion for softball, and a dedication to freedom of inquiry in the sciences. Brenda has a razor-sharp intellect which she focuses on the many experiments under her management; she is a fierce protector of the laboratory and her operators, and has the ability to work way into the night on demanding projects.

The National ESP Laboratory

During the time that I was working at PEAR I took the opportunity to participate in other research. Russell Targ, once part of the SRI remote viewing research team, and now Director of the National ESP Laboratory in Portola Valley, California, had advertized in OMNI for people to take part in associative remote viewing experiments. Experiments at SRI had found that individuals were able to accurately describe geographic locations, activities, and technical targets through the act of remote viewing, even though they were hundreds or thousands of miles away. They also speculated that the remote viewing talent was latent but could be developed with training.

Later experiments by Targ and his colleagues attempted to remotely view the silver futures on the stock exchange. Their first attempts were very successful (earning over $12,000 for their investors) but a replication failed. Targ was using a variation on remote viewing called associative remote viewing or ARV. This entailed pairing an object with an outcome. For example, "silver prices go up" might be paired with an orange. Silver prices "going down" might be paired with a toy bear. Viewers were requested to try and perceive what object would be handed to them at a certain time, when the stock options were known. In the meantime, based on the viewers' responses, usually sketches of the perceived objects, the appropriate stock would be purchased. At the end of the session, the viewers would be given feedback on their progress. ARV was first used by SRI International in remote viewing experiments aboard submarines, and by Stephan Schwartz of the Mobius Society.

Precognitive Remote Perception (PRP)

Staff at the PEAR Laboratory are not only researchers but they also act as participants in the experiments, particularly when the experiments are in the pilot stages of development. This gave me the opportunity to participate, not only in psychokinesis research but in precognitive remote experiments conducted by the lab. Through feedback on these trials I was able to sharpen my natural abilities.

The PEAR Lab has arrived at an experimental procedure that seems to be able to capture sufficient information from a target location to convince them that human consciousness is capable, with some faculty other than the five senses, of viewing a remote target.

A pair of operators decide that on a certain date and time, one of them, the "agent," will go to a geographic location, either spontaneously picked by the agent, or from information on a card picked randomly from a pool of such targets. Many controls are in place to ensure that the "percipient," the person attempting to view the scene, cannot gain information about the target by conventional means. Trials are carried out either in real-time, or they can be perceived precognitively (before the agent actually goes to the target location), or retrocognitively. Sometimes, the time delay can be anything from a few days up to several weeks, and the agent and percipient have been as far apart as opposite sides of the world. However, neither time nor distance appear to affect the outcome of the experiments.

Once at the target scene, the agent attempts to share information about the scene with the percipient, may take photographs, and completes a questionnaire that has been devised by PEAR. This questionnaire was originally in a "yes or no" binary format, about such factors as light or dark, that characterized the scene. Realizing the limitations of this format, the researchers then proceeded to a four-point scale, and finally to experiment with a sliding scale, asking questions about thirty-plus aspects of the scene. Some of these aspects, such as light and dark, are "weighted" to avoid biasing the statistics. For example, the majority of the target visits take place during daylight hours.

After viewing the scene, the participant and agent, complete identical questionnaires and these are then sent to a neutral third party, who checks that all the forms are complete. These are then passed to a researcher who adds the data into a computer and a program, specially designed for the task, and compares the two sets of responses, checking for matches and correspondences.

While I was at PEAR I was given the task of going back through all the trials that had been generated by agents and percipients, to do an "impressionistic review." For this task I rated whether there was enough similarity between the target and the perception to say, subjectively, that it was a good match. Unfortunately, most were not sufficiently matched to give them a good subjective score but there were some outstanding exceptions. In some cases, it seemed as if the percipient had almost been there with the agent and could see what the agent was seeing. Overall, however, the elements that seemed to generate good matches were targets that incorporated colorful, geometric shapes, and any kind of emotion.

While I was at PEAR I was able to travel abroad, both on vacation, to conferences, and on visits to other labs, and was able to act as both agent and percipient from England and the States, and from such exotic places as Russia and Kenya.

The Unabomber Case

One of the most intriguing projects assigned to me by Intuition Services concerned the location of the Unabomber. When I received the target in the April of 1995, I had no idea what the term Unabomber meant. However, I was able to correctly perceive his residence. I told Intuition Services: He lives in a run down piece of property surrounded by fir trees (spruces, larches)—it is a dilapidated, sort of "white trash" residence out in the countryside.

I also gave a good physical description of Theodore Kaczinsky: over six feet tall, skinny and gangly, underweight for his height, dark blond to medium brown hair, expressionless eyes, like there is no light there.

In addition, I was able to get some insight into his personality: disgruntled, cynical, spiteful, has a high intelligence and could have gone to college, may have got kicked out, feels that life has done him an injustice and feels self-righteous, that by his actions he can make a difference. I further perceived that when he hears that his bombing was successful, things go right for him and he feels vindicated, but, because nothing changes in his life resentment builds up and he bombs again. I said that part of him actually wants to get caught.

I also perceived that he could be described as an environmental terrorist but does not belong formally to any particular group. He has tried to join several groups but he usually annoys members with his opinionated babbling and they do not invite him to serious venues. I get the feeling that he works alone but has gleaned information from underground literature and groups.

This information was given to the FBI but Intuition Services was never sure whether any of this material was used in catching Kaczinsky.

Since becoming involved in serious psi research, I have learned about other remote viewing organizations, such as Mobius in California, which has included psychic archaeological excavation research in its varied projects. Also in California is the Center for Applied Intuition, (CAI) headed by William H. Krantz, which has carried out extensive intuitive business contracts.

Critics of parapsychology have repeatedly stated that the subject will only become acceptable to the scientific field when demonstrable, measurable effects can be achieved. This is now happening and practical applications of psi are becoming more evident.

Children and Remote Viewing

Children have a natural, intuitive ability which seems to diminish once they start their formal education. It is possible that this erosion of this important human ability could be curtailed by parents and educators giving credence to psi abilities in children. One researcher, who has been working with grade school children, is Dr. Yoichiro Sako, of the ESPER Laboratory, sponsored by the Sony Corporation in Japan. He presented a talk at the 1997 Society for Scientific Exploration Conference entitled "Challenging an unknown information system."

Dr. Sako presented some impressive results that he had obtained while working with grade school children in Japan. The children were able to correctly identify pictograms of words and numbers that were written on small scraps of folded paper. These scraps were then placed in the childrens' hands (or in their ear canals). The results were many times stronger than any obtained by United

States teams, with adult remote viewers. The study, if corroborated, also promises a possible method to allow remote viewers to view numbers and letters, a skill that only a few RVers have been able to master.

After hearing Dr. Sako give his talk, I asked my stepsons if they would like to try remote viewing. They agreed and I took them through some of the Inner Vision exercises, drawing and tracing. Then I gave them each a brown envelope containing a colorful picture target. I placed a blank piece of white paper over the surface of the envelope and asked them to "trace" the picture that was inside the package.

Johnathan, age 12, drew the head and neck of a bald eagle, facing to the right. He said that he could see more of the eagle but that was all he could draw. To his surprise, when we opened his envelope, there was a picture of a bald eagle in flight. Daniel, then 13, drew two small birds sitting on a wavy line. When we opened his envelope there was a picture of a mother bird feeding baby birds in a nest.

Developing Your Remote Perception Skills

First of all, let me differentiate, again, between OBE and RV. Although I came to the application of remote viewing through the practice of out-of-body experiences, they occur on different points of the same continuum. Think of a balloon, representing the matrix (the place where your information resides). On the surface of the balloon are many points of access. One person may access the information through an OBE. Another may access the information through a rigid remote viewing protocol. Yet another may use a variety of metaphysical tools, such as Tarot or I Ching. They all access the same information. It is the method or protocol that is used that is different. One method does not "fit all." That is why I teach various methods in the Inner Vision Institute courses. What follows is a "tool belt" of different methods which fall under the umbrella of Extended Remote viewing. They do not guarantee either an OBE or the immediate ability to remote view. However, practiced diligently, you should notice your innate ability improving over time.

Practical Advice to the Beginner

Whether you are studying alone, with a friend, or with a group, I hope you will find this section to be a rewarding experience for you. Before we begin, I would like to express a few thoughts:

- Remote viewing cannot be taught in its entirety in one reading. My own training has taken many years of trial and error, and the path to learning has been enriched by many teachers. However, what I hope to give you are some practical tools that you can use to practice remote viewing. The rest is up to you as an individual practitioner. Frequent practice greatly enhances the ability.

- Some professionals claim that the term, remote viewing, can only be used for laboratory-controlled studies of the phenomenon. Others feel that remote viewing has come into general usage, to denote the ability to access information from remote geographical sites using something other than the known five senses. Time and distance cease to exist, and the past and future can be accessed as easily as the present. It is this second definition, of a generalized ability, that we will be using in this section.

- Finally, the learning of remote viewing carries a certain responsibility. Use it wisely and diplomatically, as you would use any new skill.

Extended Remote Viewing or ERV

What is Extended Remote Viewing (ERV)? The term "remote viewing," according to Ingo Swann, was developed as a particular type of experimental protocol, or "control," rather than a particular type of viewing. Many RV professionals, who were trained by Swann, refer to their methodology as controlled remote viewing or CRV. Other RV groups teach variations of the more formal CRV and refer to their methods as either Technical or Scientific Remote Viewing.

ERV refers to a wider definition which includes other established RV methods such as: Associative Remote Viewing; Coordinate Remote Viewing; Future Memory; Meditative Remote Viewing; as well as precognitive remote perception (PRP) protocols. All of these techniques are valid RV methods, in the wider definition of the term. ERV has also been defined as remote reviewing using an altered state of consciousness.

Remote Perception Applications

Remote viewing can be used in many different ways. Some individuals use it solely for personal or academic research: trying to understand the mechanisms that underlie the anomalous acquisition of information. There are groups using remote viewing as an adjunct to forensic criminal work: to locate missing persons and solve crime. Some individuals use remote viewing for diagnostic work in their health-care practices. There are many applications for remote viewing.

Practical Considerations

Students of remote viewing frequently ask what techniques have been successful in initiating or developing remote viewing abilities. The following are some practical methods that have been found to be helpful. I consider the phenomenon of remote viewing to be part of our normal abilities: that it is neither occult nor paranormal but part of our human experience. It is also my belief that there are many people who have never experienced remote viewing, but who can.

First, let me dispel some fears. When an individual is remote viewing, they are in complete control and can terminate the experience whenever they want to. Most people simply visualize being back in full consciousness again. If someone disturbs you, you will just become more alert.

In the occult literature there are anecdotal stories that malevolent entities might inhabit the body while a person is off mentally traveling. I have never experienced this, although people traveling in the *astral* realms have reported contacting such entities.

However, there are some warnings. There may be a tendency for panic, denial or overconfidence when you first discover you can remote view. This is quite natural and can be overcome with curiosity and a sense of exploration and adventure. Always, remember that you are in complete control of the situation. Your physical body will continue to function. Your heart will continue to beat, you will continue to breathe, and your dinner will continue to digest. However, when you terminate the session you may experience a temporary lethargy which will lessen as you become more alert.

Beginner's Luck

You may also experience "beginners luck" (also called the Novice Effect)—the first few sessions may be spectacularly successful, to be followed by a period of time when nothing you do seems to work. This can be discouraging. Don't be deterred by this phenomenon which is called the "Serial Position Effect" and is a well-known psychological process. It happens in any new endeavor. For instance, an individual learning a new sport, such as golf, will do well in the first few games. Then, their game will drop off, only to recover as the individual persists. The drop-off is sometimes attributed to overconfidence or overenthusiasm. However, as this order of success, decline, and eventual recovery is seen in animal and mechanical studies, it may be a prevalent, universal pattern.

Questions and Answers

The following are some of the more frequently asked questions, that students ask of remote viewing, and some responses to address these questions:

- *Why do I experience fatigue upon completion of a session?* Remote viewing can be hard work and possibly uses energy reserves that are, as yet, not understood. A short nap or rest will restore your alertness.
- *I have a sense of moving through solid objects.* I have frequently experienced this. Although it feels unusual, you will soon come to accept this as an important and helpful aspect of remote viewing. It allows you access to areas where the physical body could not normally go. These are called Movement Exercises.
- *I experience sensations of rising, drifting, gaining speed, rapid travel; near destinations, I experience consciousness of changes of temperature.* Buchanan calls this experience "Perfect Site Integration or PSI" and the viewer feels as if they are actually at the site. If you are able to vocalize during this experience, to a Monitor or into a tape recorder, this is another important aspect of remote viewing

for recovering veridical information about a target. If you have an excellent memory for detail, you might record your experiences as soon as you finish the session.

- *Will I detect other remote viewers present at the target - and will they be aware that I am viewing them?* I have experienced this a few times. Most professional remote viewers report having remote viewing "companions" although the experience is difficult to corroborate.

- *Will I retain full possession of my reasoning faculties?* You will retain full reasoning faculties during a session.

- *How is remote viewing different from information picked up by someone who is psychic?* The difference is similar to that between an individual who has a natural musical talent and can "play by ear" and a trained concert pianist. The untrained musician can play beautiful music but training adds a depth and richness to the performance.

- *Is astral projection the same as remote viewing?* Astral projection is a specialized term which is applied to a metaphysical application of the Out-of-Body Experience where individuals claim to travel in the astral realm. Remote Viewing is more prosaic, accessing information about people, places and events in this dimension.

- *Are there any dangers associated with remote viewing?* Remote viewing is a normal part of our human cognitive abilities. All cultures back through the ages have reported the ability. As with any new skill, the acquisition takes discipline and practice. There are no known dangers associated with the practice of remote viewing.

- *Can I spy on people with remote viewing?* Along with RV training comes a responsibility to use it wisely and ethically.

- **Can anybody be trained to remote view?** Mostly, yes. As with any other skill, like playing the piano, most people can be trained. Some individuals, with training, can play "chopsticks" and others, with a lot of talent and training, might become concert pianists.

- **Are time and distance important in remote viewing?** Remote viewing can take you to the past, the present and the future, and distance is no obstacle. It is as easy to access information about a geographic target across the world as it is to view a nearby location.

- **I have heard about technical remote viewing, scientific remote viewing, controlled remote viewing, remote perception, extended remote viewing, coordinate remote viewing. Which is which, or are they all the same?** Basically, all of the terms used, in remote viewing training, relate to the same basic remote viewing ability. The training methods may vary according to the instructor and where they were trained. Some groups teach only one method, others, like The Inner Vision Institute, teach several methods which have a track record of success.

- **Is there any training or preparation that I should undertake before attending remote viewing training?** Any metaphysical experience is useful (meditation, TM, TMI Gateway programs) but not essential to RV training. Learning how to relax the body and focus the mind, as well as sharpening the visualization process are helpful, too.

- **Is there one technique that seems to underlie all of the known methods of remote viewing?** Over the years I have come to realize that there are certain conditions under which mental travel can occur. There has to be a certain state, a harmony between the body and the mind, a harmony of opposites. The physical body has to be relaxed and quiet, with no distractions, and the mind has to be conscious and alert. We will cover this in more detail in a later section.

The Harmony of Opposites Method

Here are some conditions that may help you carry out Extended Remote Viewing:

- A warm, comfortable environment with no undue distractions.
- A belief that you are in complete control and that you can initiate and terminate the session at will.
- A belief that remote viewing is a natural part of our human abilities—that it is an innate ability and can be trained and developed.
- Close your eyes and focus on "nothing." Exclude thoughts that interrupt and try to create a "blue space" in your imagination.
- Next, do some visualization exercises. You might want to have a friend read these to you while you have your eyes closed:

The Sense of Touch:
Imagine touching velvet, a baby bunny, sandpaper, an icecube in the palm of your hand, grains of sand.

The Sense of Smell:
Imagine smelling sweet perfume, the scent of new-mown grass, a freshly opened can of coffee, the wind off the sea.

The Sense of Hearing:
Imagine hearing a train whistle, a young baby crying, the rustle of a paper, the wind through the trees.

The Sense of Taste:
Imagine tasting a sweet candy bar, a lemon, a salty pretzel, a segment of grapefruit.

The Sense of Sight:
> Imagine seeing a flat square, then a cube, a red circle, a blue pyramid.
> Then proceed to visualizing a picture of a scene that is enjoyable to you, say a field of flowers.

- Next, as your body relaxes and your mind and imagination are busy, you may begin to feel a slight sense of disorientation. At this point say, "I want to go to _____"(and name your destination). The images you receive may be fragmented and unclear but with time and practice they will resolve into clearer, more whole pictures. Remember to practice, practice, practice.

Example

When I was working in New Jersey I lived in a three story house. My landlady gave me permission to borrow a bed-frame that was stored in the attic. Bringing the bed-frame down the narrow attic stairs, it got stuck. I reasoned that somebody had got it up to the attic, so I should be able to bring it down. I did a remote viewing and saw two burly young men carrying the bed-frame, at a certain angle, up the attic stairs. I terminated the RV and pushed the frame into the angle I saw and it came easily down the stairs.

- A good exercise, to gain experience with remote viewing, is to choose an event that has recently occurred and then watch the news media for further information.

First, try to actively daydream. Then direct your consciousness to view a chosen target. (Be ethical and do not intrude on the privacy of others.) Record your impressions and try to verify what you see. Try RVing your alarm clock before you open your eyes in the morning (or if you awaken at night). Set yourself the target before you go to sleep at night. You will not always reach your target. It takes time, practice, and more practice.

Example

I was appalled by the murder of Ennis Cosby, the son of actor Bill Cosby. Young Ennis had been shot while changing a tire at the side of the road. I did a remote viewing exercise to locate the murder scene. I saw a truck come by with two young men. The man who was driving was a thin-faced man. I described him as weasel-faced. The other man had a baby-face and was softer, rounder in appearance. The truck stopped. There were taunts. The thin man leaned on the shoulder of the fat man and fired at Ennis, then drove on. A few weeks later the thin man was caught and my description of the weasel-faced appearance seemed to fit the accused man.

- Try and remote view the front page of the next day's newspaper. There is usually a major color picture on the front page. Check your perceptions when you actually get the paper.

Example

As part of a class exercise, the group remote viewed a colored picture that would be prominent on the front page of the next day's local newspaper. One individual visualized a red setting sun. The next day, feedback from the newspaper revealed a photo of a laser light show, in a downtown area of Las Vegas, depicting a cowboy and cowgirl riding a horse into a red sunset.

- When you know that you are going to visit a new location, remote view it and record your impressions. Later, when you actually visit the location, you can check the accuracy of your perceptions.

Remote Tracking

Cooperate with a friend to do this exercise in remote tracking. As this exercise could invade the privacy of another person, do it with mutual respect and permission. The "outbound experimenter" leaves the house (after synchronizing watches with the "perceiver") and walks or drives around the neighborhood, for about twenty minutes. Every few minutes the "outbounder" records his impressions into a small hand-held tape recorder what they are seeing, hearing, thinking, etc. Look for interesting and unusual events, people and things. You could even take instant pictures, if you are keeping a permanent record of your progress.

Back at the house, the "perceiver" attempts to remote view where the "outbounder" is, what he or she is seeing, thinking and doing. The "perceiver" writes down his or her impressions, making drawings, diagrams etc. Try and time the perceptions, writing down the time next to the impressions. When the "outbounder" returns, the two of you should compare notes and times. You will be surprised at the matches.

Example

The most significant part of the RV week (according to one Inner Vision student) was the remote tracking project. For 20 minutes I tried to "track" where he went. I was to draw pictures of what "he" saw and record results. The accuracy of this was not perfect but it was close enough to be shocking. The closest I can come to describing this is how you can "see and feel" someone you are close to. But this was done in a controlled environment, on demand, with someone I had just met. At times, I could sense emotion combined with the visuals I was getting from him. The other student also had incredible results when I went out and he "tracked" me. The most incredible hit was when he accurately saw me petting a dog and then describing it "marking its territory" (yes the dog did its thing and he "saw" it).

Coordinate Remote Viewing

Have a colleague go through an atlas and pick out geographic places at random. Look in the index of the atlas and write down the coordinates of each location on an index card. Some people have trouble with actual longitude and latitude coordinates. They switch into logical mode and try to reason out where the location is. To overcome this problem, write down the number and letter coordinates of each location, B4 or G6, for example, instead of the latitude and longitude. Some students feel that they can use imagery to carry out this exercise. For example, imagine a spinning globe of the Earth. Imagine your finger coming closer and closer to the globe. Then stop the globe with an imaginary finger, saying "There," and look at where you have arrived. Another option is to give the student a random number which has been linked by a third party to a chosen geographical location.

The Ritual Method

Most ritual methods are based on imagery, concentration and relaxation. Most begin with some cleansing and purifying ritual such as bathing, herbal scents in the form of oils and candles, certain dietary restrictions, and metaphysical tools such as tarot cards or crystal balls.

Tattwa cards are one aid to remote viewing. They make use of symbolic color-keys to unlock the doorways of the mind. The Tattwas are colored geometrical figures, used in some schools of the Indian Tantric sect, to symbolize the elements of earth, air, fire and water. The five Tattwas consist of the following:

- Tejas (fire) - represented by a red equilateral triangle;
- Prithivi (earth) - a yellow square;
- Apas (water) - a silver lunar crescent lying on its back;
- Vayu (air) - a greenish-blue circle;
- Akasa (astral light or spirit) - a blackish-violet egg.

From these five Mother-Tattwas were formed another twenty sub-Tattwas, which were formed by placing a smaller version on one particular Tattwa, on top of one of the other four Tattwas. The adept would make his or her own twenty-five Tattwa cards and select one of them for his experimental projection. He or she would stare at the chosen card until no other factor was present in his consciousness. Then, in the mind's eye, the individual would imaginatively transform the card into a vast door, or sometimes an embroidered curtain, will the door to swing open, and then pass through it in imagination, there to experience a vision.

Most of those who have experienced this technique have claimed that the nature of the astral vision bears an authentic relationship to the symbol employed—if one uses the water Tattwa, one usually experiences a watery vision and that as one goes on using the technique the visions become less dream-like and more real.

Example

As a class exercise I drew the card with symbols depicting the Earth and Spirit. I stared at the card until some visual distortions occurred. I knew that these distortions were normal visual after-effects. The images seemed to become three dimensional, colors shifted—lights becoming darker, dark colors becoming lighter, I could see a shadow of the dark areas if I shifted my gaze. At this point I closed my eyes and saw the after image of the square as a doorway. I seemed to go towards the doorway and passed through into a visualization of the Earth with its corona of light. The corona appeared to be the spirit of the Earth.

Technical Aids

Sometimes, technical aids are worth obtaining, if only to show you what state of consciousness you need to be in to remote view. Altered states of consciousness do not come easily, in fact, there are some people whose only states are awake or asleep. If they try to meditate they fall asleep.

Technical aids come in many types depending on your goal. There are books and tapes available to enable you to achieve physical relaxation, and there are tapes, programs and technical devices to enable a person to enter different mental states. Many of these are described in advertisements in New Age and metaphysical journals. However, they caution that these devices should not be used by anybody who suffers from epilepsy because the flashing lights can precipitate a seizure.

The Monroe Method

The first recommended method could also be called the hypnogogic method, as it entails slipping into an altered state; as one enters that borderline, often visual, state between sleeping and waking. I also recommended trying to achieve a "vibrational" state from which to launch into a session.

Condition A: Vibrational State: Monroe Method

Monroe suggests lying down in a comfortable position in a darkened room with your head pointing to magnetic north. Loosen your clothing but stay warm. Do not set time limitations and make arrangements so that you will not be disturbed. Repeat five times to yourself:

> *I will consciously perceive and remember all that I encounter during this relaxation procedure. I will recall in detail when I am completely awake only those matters which will be beneficial to my physical and mental well-being.*

Begin breathing through your half-open mouth and slip into that state bordering sleep. It might be helpful to keep one arm in the air, as it falls it will awaken you. Or you could concentrate on an object; as other images come into your mind, watch them.

This technique is very similar to one used by Thomas Edison, the New Jersey inventor. Edison would often catnap during the day in his office chair, holding a handful of marbles. On the floor under his chair would be a metal tray and, as he fell into borderline sleep, his hand would relax, letting go the marbles, with a loud noise, which would wake him up. Frequently, upon waking, he would have the solution to a problem or a new idea which had been generated in the hypnogogic state.

Condition B: Monroe Method

Begin to clear your mind and observe your field of vision through closed eyes. Note light patterns (these are naturally occurring phosphenes and harmless). Watch until they disappear.

Condition C: Monroe Method

This state involves a complete state of physical relaxation where all sense of awareness with the body is lost. There is no awareness of sensory input from the body. The only source of stimulation is your own thoughts.

Condition D: Monroe Method

Condition D is induced from a rested or refreshed state and not the result of normal fatigue. It can be practiced in the morning or after a short nap. With the eyes closed, focus on a spot in the blackness about a foot from your forehead. Concentrate your consciousness on that spot. Move it about three feet away, then six feet. Rotate the spot ninety degrees above your head. Mentally, reach for the "vibrations" at that spot and pull them into your head.

Monroe recommends smoothing or "pulsing" out the vibrations. Next, reach out an arm to grasp an object which you know is out of normal reach. Feel the object and let your hand pass through it, before bringing it back. Then, stopping the vibrations, checking the actual location of the object.

Full Separation: Monroe Method

Monroe advocates the "lift-put" method. Think of getting lighter and how nice it would be to float upwards. An alternative is the "rotation" technique. Turn over in bed, twisting first the top of the body, head and shoulders until you turn right over and float upwards. Monroe adds that a wide variety of experiences are yours for the taking.

Meditation Method

The basic state of meditation, which consists of relaxation and concentration, plus a little imagery, is the ideal state in which to remote view. In fact, many people have claimed to have spontaneously viewed a location while they were meditating or practicing yoga.

There are many types of meditation but they generally have the same goals; of achieving relaxation and improving concentration. One of these methods is the concentration or focusing meditation, where the individual concentrates on an image such as a flower, a candle flame, a word or mantra, or the sound of their own breathing. Insightful meditation, or mindfulness, aims at focusing the mind on a concept such as peace or love to attain transcendental awareness. Chakra meditation focuses on energizing the flow of psychic energy up the body through the seven Chakra centers. The vibrational sensations often encountered during such practice may be a precursor to a state where remote viewing may occur. If the experience does not come naturally during the meditation state it can be encouraged by adding visualization techniques.

The Christos Technique

Australian journalist G.M. Glaskin wrote *Windows of the Mind* in 1974 in which he described a technique for enabling human consciousness to separate from the physical body and travel to distant locations. His system involves a series of exercises during which the subject becomes relaxed and the sense of body image becomes slightly distorted and disoriented. Next, imagery is employed to enable the subject to perceive locations distant in time and space.

The technique employs three people, the subject and two helpers. One helper sits at the subject's head and, with the soft ball of the fist, firmly massages the subject's forehead in a circular fashion. The other helper firmly massages the subject's ankles. This continues for between five to fifteen minutes.

Next, one helper instructs the subject in various visualization exercises during which the subject imagines first the legs extending and getting longer, then returning to normal, then the arms and head doing the same. This proceeds until the subject feels like he has grown about two or three feet.

After the stretching imaging, the subject visualizes his own front door, taking care to look closely at all its features, and verbalizes what he sees. The helper then takes the subject mentally up above his house to visualize the location from a height. The subject is instructed to change the time of day from dark to sunny and back again so that he feels that he has complete control of the situation.

The subject is then instructed to fly up above the clouds, to travel and to come down somewhere else. The helper then asks the subject, "Look at your feet. What do you have on your feet?" From then on the helper questions the subject as they proceed through the scene, which may be from his current or past life. The subject usually terminates the scene himself and returns to the present in a relaxation back to normal.

The Imagery Method

Muldoon and Carrington, two early researchers, advocated the use of imagery as one of the triad of conditions necessary for the phenomenon to occur along with relaxation and concentration. They suggested the following imagery:

- The image of floating off the bed, moving upright and traveling away from the room. They advised the novice to practice, practice, practice.
- To imagine a duplicate of yourself standing in front of you with its back to you. Observe this image. Observe the posture, dress, and other features. Ask

yourself "Who am I?" and "Where am I?" Transfer your consciousness to the double image of yourself.

Ophiel's "Little System"

In 1961 Ophiel devised a technique for remote perception which used a combination of memory and visualization.

- Pick a familiar route between two rooms in your house.
- Memorize every detail of it.
- Choose six points along the route and look at these points for several minutes every day. Symbols, scents, and sounds play a role creating associations with the route and reinforce the image.
- Lie down and relax while you try to project to the first point. Move from point to point.
- Later, extend your projection past your route.

Ophiel points out that you may hears strange noises during these exercises but they are only mental static and should be ignored.

Associative Remote Viewing (ARV)

The following example uses a variation of remote viewing techniques called associative remote viewing (ARV) as used in experiments by Russell Targ. My husband Dave and I tried this variation of ARV to predict the outcome of a major football game.

Example

Dave chose four dissimilar objects to represent four outcomes:

Item #1:that Team A would win by a small margin;
Item #2:that Team A would win by a large margin;
Item #3:that Team B would win by a small margin;
Item #4:that Team B would win by a large margin.

The results of the game would be known at eight o'clock on that Saturday night so, during the day, I tried to view which object Dave would hand me at the end of the game. I drew two objects and gave the drawings to him to keep until later. We decided not to bet on that particular game but we could have. What I drew was a circular object with a spoke through the middle, then I deliberately drew the circular object again in more definition; it looked like a donut.

When the outcome of the game was announced, Dave handed me a round reel of electrical tape, the object he had chosen to represent team A winning by a large margin. However, I had also drawn the spoke, which Dave said was representative of another object, a stick, that he had chosen to represent Team B winning by a small margin, so we didn't count this experiment as a total success.

Future Memory Technique

In 1989 I corresponded with another future viewer, James Van Avery, and learned about his Future Memory technique. Van Avery was a Senior Electronics Design Specialist for a major Aerospace Company in Seattle, Washington and he had studied and participated in the paranormal phenomena of remote viewing for more than fifteen years. During those years he had developed a technique that could remote view not only the present and past, but could look into the future using a concept he called Future Memory. Like a fly-fisherman casting his lure into the water, Van Avery suggests sending conscious thought ahead of the event that is to be accessed and then perceiving the images that arise. Future Memory combines imagination with the memory recall system. By incorporating normal memory and shifting consciousness to the future, Van Avery believes that anybody can be vividly aware of future events.

Van Avery's method starts off much the same as all the other methods in that the viewer should select a quiet, warm location where they can remain undisturbed for some length of time. Next come visualization exercises which focus on memorizing your immediate surroundings, followed by visualization of objects that are not immediately apparent such as the woodgrain inside furniture and the inside of a flower bud.

The next step in the process entails reflecting on how your mind works. Van Avery feels it is important to become aware of your own personal way of keeping track of information in your head. He stresses keeping records of your progress through these exercises and to draw the targets with lots of detail. When viewing a target, notice patterns and shape rather than function.

Van Avery suggests an interesting exercise: collect a stack of about twenty colorful magazines and a sketch pad. Ask yourself what is on the next page and sketch your perception before turning to see what the page actually contains. Look for contrasts in shapes and forms of light and dark.

Next comes the fly-fisherman trick. Send your consciousness into the future, ahead of the event that you want to view, and use your memory skills to access information about this event. Van Avery feels that the hardest part of these exercises is changing your belief system to accommodate the fact that these skills are possible.

Controlled Remote Viewing

There are now manuals for CRV currently available to the public, but the protocol can only be taught by someone already trained to the teacher level. However, the following comparative points, which refer to Stages I-III of CRV, as taught by Paul Smith of RVIS, will help the beginning student understand CRV training.

There are many similarities between controlled remote viewing (CRV) and extended remote viewing (ERV). For example:

- Both CRV and ERV encourage movement exercises, that is, moving around the target to access further sensory and dimensional information.
- Motion at the target site is often perceived in both CRV and ERV.
- Both CRV and ERV focus, in the early stages, on accessing sensory data.
- In CRV a "cool-down" period prior to accessing the signal line is optional: ERV utilizes a series of exercises to quiet the physical body and focus the mind, "the harmony of opposites."
- Sketching is a necessary part of CRV, as it also is in ERV.
- Sensory information is accessed in both CRV and ERV (touch, taste, smell, sight, and hearing).
- In ERV, negative states such as fatigue, illness and stress, are known to decrease the efficiency of remote viewing; in CRV, personal inclemencies, such as worries or illness, are stated up front.

There are also differences between CRV and ERV, for example:

- In CRV the student is encouraged to access the Matrix (the place of origin of the target information) from a point outside the Matrix. In ERV, the student is considered an integral part of the Matrix.

- In CRV, the student "quits on high"—takes a break when they have success with a target. In ERV, the student is able to switch between techniques.
- In CRV the student is not seen as entering an obvious altered state of consciousness, while in ERV an altered state of consciousness is encouraged.
- The teaching of CRV is done in an authoritarian style with obvious teacher/student roles. ERV is taught in a more democratic style.
- CRV is very structured; in fact the structure is considered the most important part of the process. ERV is less structured and more relaxed.
- In ERV the target is the most important part of the process; in CRV the structure (how the student acquires the signal line) is considered more important.
- In ERV, target information can be recorded on anything (white or colored paper, computer record, drawing pad); in CRV the information from the target is hand-drawn and written on blank, white sheets of paper. This is not an absolute but is encouraged, to limit the amount of environmental overlay.
- In CRV, there is a theory that the central nervous system acts as a receiver for the signal line; in ERV, human consciousness is thought to access the data about the target.
- Perfect Site Integration (PSI) and Bilocation (where the student feels they are in full sensory contact with the site) is discouraged in CRV; it is encouraged in ERV.
- In CRV, the Monitor and Tasker are considered essential components of the RV process during training. However, according to Paul Smith, CRV can just as easily be done solo, and, in fact, most operational sessions are done that way. In ERV, monitors are sometimes used during training but, mostly, the viewer works alone.

- In stages I-III CRV training, the monitor is aware of the target during the training session and gives feedback to the student, such as "correct, cannot feedback, etc." Later, both the monitor and student are blind to the target. In ERV both the instructor and student are blind to the target until the feedback stage is reached.
- CRV is excellent for accessing a great deal of sensory and sketched data. However, sometimes, despite having correctly identified the sensory data and drawn sketches that match the target, the student cannot identify the target. In the Fort Meade unit, the data that was collected by the viewers was evaluated by analysts to extract useable information. ERV students can mostly identify their target and are encouraged to do so.
- Much more sensory data is provided through CRV and multiple sketches are made that "morph" and progress in complexity until they appear to match the target. In ERV, students access the information mostly through "chunks" of visualization and other sensory information.
- CRV is probably a good method for individuals who prefer a lot of structure in the learning process. ERV might be a good introduction to CRV, in that it encourages and strengthens sensory access and drawing skills

In summary, I feel that in CRV I have a valuable addition to my repertoire of RV skills. CRV and ERV are highly complementary methods. One of the most positive aspects of having this repertoire is that different techniques can be applied to varied applications.

For the student contemplating training in CRV, the following observations from a CRV Basic Course might be helpful in helping them to decide which method is best for them.

Prior to the CRV Course you need to put aside all that you had learned about remote viewing, in order to fully participate in the CRV process. Paul Smith recommends a bibliography of reading materials and suggestions for additional preparation for the course. He suggests taking a basic drawing course, if the student was not artistically inclined. He could also have recommended that students practice their handwriting skills, as these constituted a major part of the course. Many of us are so used to tapping out our notes and essays on a computer keyboard and there is a lot of hand written note-taking and essay writing included in the CRV course. Paul explained that there is a reason behind this practice. Writing with the hand helps imprint the material and concepts of CRV more firmly into consciousness.

RVIS's course kicks off with a 12-hour day of work in the classroom, where the students cover the history of RV, key people in the field, the theory and rationale behind CRV, and an introduction to Stage I. When I took the class, it was taught in a traditional style, from the front of the class, with the instructor writing salient points on a whiteboard. Students were expected to take extensive notes, which were then used to write essays on the material. Paul Smith teaches from his copy of the original CRV Manual, that was developed by him at Fort Meade for the Army. Our written notes were supposed to be sufficient take-away information. I felt that I was pretty much able to keep up with the note-taking but perhaps older students, or those out of school for a long time, might find the task more difficult. I know that I finished that first day with writer's cramp.

During the class sessions, students were taught the fundamentals of CRV, up to Stage III. Each stage was preceded by theory, note-taking, essay writing, and only then did we get to do practice sessions. Prior to Stage II, which involves the acquisition of sensory data, we took an early morning trip to Red Rock Canyon to immerse ourselves in the sights, sounds, smells, tastes, touch, and dimensionals of this beauty spot. By Stage III, we were sketching our perceptions and writing target summaries. Basic training is not finished before the student has completed ten further practice sessions, either alone or with a monitor. These are mailed to the student after the class and feedback is provided at each stage. Paul also offers Intermediate, Advanced and Teacher Training Courses.

Review of Methods

It must seem confusing for a beginner to have to decide from the various techniques presented in this section; but, if you just remember the three necessary conditions—relaxation, concentration, and imagery—and aim for a harmony of opposites—relaxed body and active mind—you should be able to remote view a distant location. However, it takes lots of patience. Then, with practice, you may be able to put the ability to practical use in remote viewing.

Educational Courses in Parapsychology

Students often ask how they can become involved in parapsychology research and what educational courses they can pursue to become employed in the field. I often have to disappoint them. As mentioned elsewhere, actual funding for parapsychology in America has been abysmal. Private sponsors have kept the field afloat but more and more research groups are disappearing. The McDonnell Laboratory in St. Louis, MO, and the Psychophysical Research Laboratory run by Charles Honorton in Princeton, both funded by the McDonnell Foundation, have closed. As has Science Unlimited Research Foundation, another psi laboratory, which ran for several years in San Antonio. The early government work on remote viewing at the Stanford Research Institute, appears to have officially ceased. The only major United States laboratories, where psi is still currently under study, are the PEAR Laboratory at Princeton University, the Institute for Parapsychology at FRNM in Durham, North Carolina, and the Mind-Science Foundation in San Antonio, Texas. There are almost no new parapsychology research positions. Additionally, there are only a few conventional educational institutes that will allow a student to major in parapsychology. Two of the most forward in this field are Saybrook Graduate School and Rosebridge Graduate School, both in California. In most undergraduate education, the study of unconventional topics is discouraged, particularly if the student is going on to graduate studies. The majority of graduate colleges do not look favorably at a transcript that lists parapsychological topics.

However, having said that, there are several avenues that a student can take to become educated in parapsychology. The first is to carry on a parallel process of public and private education. During the time the student is carrying out their conventional education, they can be reading many of the books available on parapsychology. Organizations such as FRNM in Durham, N.C., would welcome student enquiries for reading suggestions. Students should not only read books giving a favorable opinion of parapsychology but should also read the critical reviews.

The interested student should join organizations such as Parapsychological Association (PA) and the American Society for Psychical Research (ASPR) in New York, to keep abreast of the latest research in the field. In addition, the ASPR has an extensive library of book and journals which is made available to interested students.

Individuals should also subscribe to the journals documenting parapsychology research, such as the *Journal of Parapsychology*, the *Journal of the American Society for Psychical Research*, and the *Journal of Scientific Exploration*, as well as the *Skeptical Inquirer*, (the journal of the Committee for the Scientific Investigation of Claims of the Paranormal, CSICOP).

Each year there are three or four professional meetings and conventions that these societies hold around the country. Students and interested individuals should make an effort to attend these, to hear talks on new research and to meet and network with psi researchers.

Dr. Rhea White, founder of Parapsychological Sources of Information, Inc. (PSI, Inc.) and editor of *Parapsychological Abstracts International*, has compiled a chronological world-wide listing of degrees conferred in part for a thesis or dissertation on parapsychology. Her listing contains 227 doctoral programs, 101 master's programs, plus another 8 items for miscellaneous other degrees. Dr. White found that 1981 was a peak year for psi dissertations and theses and that American education institutions led the field, followed then by England, Germany, Italy, India, Scotland, the Republic of South Africa, and the Netherlands.

Regarding individual schools, she estimated that City College of the City University of New York led the field, followed by John F. Kennedy University in California. Next, in terms of numbers of dissertations and theses, came the University of Freiburg in Germany, the University of Edinburgh in Scotland, Saybrook in California, Duke University in North Carolina, Andhra University in India, and California State University. Other colleges which occasionally granted degrees in psi topics have included New York University, Union Graduate School, United States International University, and the University of Ultrecht, then in decreasing order of frequency, Boston University, California School of Professional Psychology, Catholic University of America, Harvard University, University of London, Columbia University, Fuller Theological Seminary, Oxford University, University of Pennsylvania, University of the Philippines, the University of Surrey, Lund University, University of Cambridge, University of Chicago, University of Chile, and University of Texas at Austin.

While this list appears impressive it must be remembered that it covers one hundred years of education and that some institutions have since closed. In addition, it is important to find not only a school which will permit a student to undertake such a project, but the student also needs to find dissertation committee members willing to put their careers on the line in advocating such a project.

Becoming Involved in Psi Research

Occasionally, in publications such as *Omni*, researchers will put out a call for volunteer subjects for psi research. This was one of the initial ways that I was able to become actively involved. Sometimes this involvement is through the mail and the student participates through questionnaires and surveys, or as an active remote subject in psychokinesis or remote viewing exercises. There is rarely any pay for this type of participation, but being actively involved in an interesting project is often reward enough.

At other times, a research center will publish a request for volunteers who can visit the research center and participate on-site. The PEAR Lab has recruited many of its operators through word-of-mouth, and through articles that have been written about the laboratory. Most laboratories are not looking for gifted subjects, although some, such as PRL, sought out participants who fulfilled certain characteristics, such as predetermined personality traits, prior training in meditation, and previous paranormal experiences.

The Institute for Parapsychology holds a six-week residential Summer School in Durham, N.C. where qualified applicants can study and interact with major researchers in the psi field. Also the Princeton Engineering Anomalies Research Laboratory at Princeton University has initiated a Summer Institute consisting of lectures and classes with distinguished researchers in the anomalies field.

Even though there are very few actual paying jobs in the parapsychology field, there are many ways that the interested individual can become involved.

References

Dunne, B.J., and J.P. Bisaha. 1979. "Precognitive remote viewing in the Chicago area." *Journal of Parapsychology.* 43: 17–30.

Dunne, B.J., R.G. Jahn, and R.D. Nelson. 1983. *Precognitive remote perception.* Technical Note PEAR 83003. Princeton University Engineering Anomalies Research, Princeton University, School of Engineering/Applied Science.

Honorton, C., P. Barker, M.P. Varvoglis, R.E. Berger, and E.I. Schechter. 1985. First timers: An exploration of factors affecting psi Ganzfeld performance. Presented paper at the 28th Annual Convention of the Parapsychological Association.

Presentation given by Albert Stubblebine at the International Symposium on UFO Research (sponsored by the International Association for new Science) in Denver, Co. May 22-25, 1992, on the subject of "Remote Viewing as a Research Tool." Quoted from V. Johnson "The Aviary, the Aquarium and Eschatology in CE Chronicles:

The Journal of the Close Encounters Research network."
Nov/Dec. 1993.

Targ, R. 1987. "The National ESP Test Instructions." 93–24.
Published by the National ESP Laboratory, Portola Valley, California.

Section
Two

APPENDIX A

ALTERED STATES OF CONSCIOUSNESS

A Rose By Any Other Name

Historical and anthropological accounts of OBEs have been described by many terms according to the culture or discipline relating them. From spiritual science we have the term astral projection and spirit travel; the Ayawasca ritual from the North American Indians speak of "loosing the bounds of the soul;" the Egyptians called the phenomenon Ba; Jacqui Indians refer to Brujo or "witch flying"; Tibetan writings talk of "displacing the soul" and the "power of the Delog"; the Greeks termed the ability "ecstasy"; African Zulus described OBEs as "opening the gates of distance"; and the Australian Aborigines as "seeing at a distance"; in shamanic terminology OBEs were thought to be induced by the "ritual of the irrational;" and from Indian teachings we learn of the ability being called samadhi, sidhi powers, and trong jug.

In recent times, the OBE has been known by other names, such as bilocation, cataleptic states, dissociation, doppelganger, ecsomatic experience, exteriorization, mental imagery, mobile center of consciousness, remote viewing, remote perception, and traveling clairvoyance. Only three major terms are now used regularly by researchers of the phenomenon: out-of-body experiences (OBEs or OOBEs), remote viewing, and remote perception.

There is a confusion over the definitions of out-of-body experience and remote viewing, whether they are the same or different aspects of the same experience. Historically and culturally, OBEs and distant viewing appeared to have been complementary human faculties. For example a native Australian would go out-of-body, travel to a distant location where he or she would access information that would be of practical use to his community. However, in modern times, scientific methods have been used to study various aspects of this ability and the two phenomena of OBEs and remote perception/remote viewing have come to be seen as two distinct entities with a great deal of grey area in between.

The term "remote viewing" was first coined in 1971 by Ingo Swann and Janet Mitchell, along with Karlis Osis and Gertrude Schmeidler, at the American Society for Psychical Research. When Swann was invited, in late 1972, to participate in psi experiments at the Stanford Research Institute, he took the concept of remote viewing with him and it was adopted by Puthoff and Targ as a working definition. According to Puthoff and Targ in their classic 1976 paper entitled "A Perceptual Channel for Information Transfer over Kilometer Distances":

> As observed in the laboratory, the basic phenomenon appears to cover a range of subjective experiences variously referred to in the literature as autoscopy (in the medical literature); exteriorization or dissociation (psychological literature); simple clairvoyance, traveling clairvoyance, or out-of-body experience (parapsychological literature); or astral projection (occult literature). We choose the term "remote viewing" as a neutral descriptive term, free from prior associations and bias as to mechanism.

The SRI group initially headed by physicist Hal Puthoff, and later joined by Russell Targ and others, implemented remote viewing into their experimental protocols. Swann's definition of remote viewing is that it is a mixture of what used to be called clairvoyance, thought transference, and telepathy. It is a process where a viewer perceives information about a distant location using "something" other than the known five senses.

What came to be called the "out-bound experimenter" model by SRI was designed and implemented between 1971 and 1972, at the ASPR, with Swann as subject, Janet Mitchell as monitor, and Osis and Schmeidler as supervisors. In the "out-bound experimenter" model, a viewer would try to perceive the whereabouts of a researcher who had gone to a local target, say a park or museum. Vera Feldman and Erlander Harraldson were the first two modern "out-bound experimenters." Swann's book *Everybody's Guide to Natural ESP* documents the early history of remote viewing research and the problems encountered in researching this controversial topic.

Since the early research at the American Society for Psychical Research (ASPR) and, later, at the Stanford Research Institute (SRI), the term remote viewing has come into general usage, usually to denote the ability to perceive hidden or remote information by anomalous or psychic means.

Business Applications

It has only been in the past two decades that controlled experimental protocols have been designed specifically to explore OBEs and remote perception. Since then, several commercial groups have been applying remote viewing on a practical basis; offering to remote view for business, industry, and government. Their efforts have shown a significant degree of success. According to these groups remote viewing is a learnable skill.

A Rebirth of Human Consciousness

After decades of deliberate neglect, the topic of human consciousness is once again coming under scientific scrutiny. Discussions on the topic are now appearing in respected psychology literature. Is it too late to salvage consciousness as a viable area of research or are we entering an exciting new era of investigation? What are the problems that have hindered the progress of consciousness research and can we implement innovative approaches in its recovery? Several major problems—diversity of definitions, paradigmatic change, and theoretical development—have all contributed to the lack of progress.

One of the earliest references to consciousness was William James' "function of knowing"; descriptive definitions of consciousness have been given by Margaret Mead (social origins of individual consciousness); by Duval and Wicklund (objective self-awareness); by Natsoulas (mutual knowledge, internal knowledge, awareness, direct awareness, perceptual unity, waking consciousness and double consciousness); and by Baruss who has given us a further twenty-nine definitions.

However, these definitions do not provide an adequate description of total consciousness, nor can they address the problem that consciousness is, in essence, an individual phenomenon and suffers the same problems of definition as emotional concepts such as love and hate. Maybe, because of the personal and individual nature of consciousness, a precise and consistent definition of consciousness may not be possible.

During the end of the last century consciousness was considered to be the undisputed subject matter of classical psychology which, at that time, considered sense-data (sensory manifestations of consciousness) to be the foundation of all mental life. This paradigm existed until the taboo on introspection led psychologists to abandon consciousness as the subject of psychology in favor of research into behavior.

Behaviorism is a radical form of objective psychology in which all references to introspection and consciousness are rejected in favor of a discussion of physiologically relevant events primarily in terms of stimulus and response. Since then, theories of consciousness have been viewed from several perspectives: as an evolutionary or developmental process (Jaynes); as being a product of language development (LeDoux, Wilson & Gazzaniga); and a function of the divided brain (Ornstein).

There is no lack of theory to explain consciousness. However, the theories that are available are diffuse and orthogonal, and there seems to be little common bond between them. What may be needed is an integrative key which will clarify their differences and combine their advantages.

Facilitating Altered States of Consciousness

There seem to be certain channels through which the individual can enter a state of altered consciousness. In this altered state the ability to have an OBE increases. Many orthodox remote viewers state that their CRV protocols do not require an altered state but this claim has not yet been tested. When Swann's brain wave states were tested at the ASPR in New York, it was found that he entered a state of light sleep. It is possible that CRV takes place in a waking state, with dips into slower brain rhythms.

In 1957 Woodburn Heron reported that the visual phenomena of subjects undergoing sensory deprivation

were similar to those experienced after taking the intoxi-
cating drug of the mescal plant, which is a ceremonial
practice of some Indian tribes in the Southwest.

Heron's subjects drew sketches of the imagery and
sensations that they experienced during sensory deprivation experiments and some subjects reported OBE-like
sensations. Some subjects reported that they felt as if
another body were lying beside them in the cubicle, and
in one case the bodies overlapped, partly occupying the
same space. Others reported feelings of otherness or body
strangeness. When trying to describe their sensations,
some said, "my mind seemed to be a ball of cotton wool
floating over my body" or "something seemed to be sucking
my mind out through my eyes."

Cultural Considerations

John Whitman, writing in *The Psychic Power of Plants*,
said that the concept of being able to move from one's
physical body to travel through space to distant points is
an ancient one often connected with sacred ceremonies
and the use of hallucinogenic plants to reach a different
state of reality. The idea that a non-physical body, often
called the soul or "psyche," could move rapidly through
time and space was a traditional belief of the rational
Greeks and most ancient cultures. The Greeks reported
that the soul was capable of moving from the flesh to gather
useful information, either from another place on earth or
from the underworld.

Siberian tribes, generally ones using the hallucinogenic
mushroom, amanita muscaria, also maintained this belief.
They reported a person's ability to have "out of the body"
experiences if they had mastered both their physical and
spiritual selves. Since this was considered to be extremely
difficult, OBEs were usually accomplished only by the

shaman who had reached a higher level of consciousness than the other members of the tribe. According to Whitman, the ability gave him the power to see objects in far-away places.

Both Wasson and Castaneda described having OBEs. Wasson in consulting the sacred mushroom in Mexico reported that his soul seemed to soar in an instant. Castaneda, through his apprenticeship to the Yaqui Indian, Don Juan, described his OBEs after eating sacred mushrooms as "a separation of the soul from the body, which seemed like a lump of clay lying below oneself." Like Wasson, he too soared into the air. He reported being able to push himself skyward with a gentle springing motion, only to find himself gliding on his back through a dark sky with clouds passing him by. He had a sense of extraordinary speed and feeling of complete freedom of movement so that he could fly in circles with control over time and space.

As mentioned in the last chapter, the use of sacred ceremonies and hallucinogenic plants in rituals to produce OBEs have been practiced by cultures such as the Mexican Indians and Siberian shamans. The use of "sacred mushrooms" in Central and South America has been described by several writers. Hallucinogenic plants can cause a separation between the mind and the body resulting in the ability to travel outside of the body, and descriptions of these ceremonies have been well documented.

During the 18th and 19th centuries, explorers found that the Turanian and Mongolian cultures of Siberia practiced a form of Shamanism and through the practice of dancing, meditation, fasting, and the use of hallucinogenic plants the shaman could enter an altered state of consciousness. In this altered state he could "see" what was happening in different places. The shaman could travel out-of-body and perceive events not ordinarily received by the five senses. According to shamanic literature, during an OBE the shaman could travel both to earthly places and to the world of the dead.

Certain plants are also used by the Amazon Indians to achieve OBEs. The Ayawasca is a vine with a narcotic sap which is capable of causing hallucinations and delirium. This plant is used in the Ayawasca ritual, a magical, religious ceremony and, it is said that the plant enables the taker to leave the body and travel to distant locations and divine the future.

According to pagan tradition, witches rubbed their bodies with herbal extracts of aconite, belladonna and hemlock, and were able to experience mental flight. The ability to leave the body at will was part of a witch's repertoire of skills.

OBEs and near-death experiences (NDE) have frequently been termed hallucinations, imagination, and fantasy. There are, however, differences between drug-induced hallucinations and the images seen during spontaneous OBEs. For example, experiencers have commented that perceptual objects in the OBE are organized and coherent, rather than the fragmented, isolated images seen during drug ingestion.

Much has been written about the use of plants and plant extracts to induce an altered states of consciousness. Most produce dramatic changes in visual perception, including distinctive visions, which are referred to as hallucinations. But, no matter how compelling the visions, the perceiver does not usually mistake them for reality. The effects of the hallucinogens can vary depending on when, where, why and, most importantly, by whom the drug is ingested. However, certain subjective effects are commonly reported. Visually, most subjects experience an increase in the vividness of colors and in the beauty of the physical world, and with their eyes shut view a constantly changing display. Often there are complex auditory experiences, such as conversations between imaginary people, or music, and there are a variety of imagined odors, tastes and bodily sensations. However, ingesting drugs is not necessarily needed to experience these effects. They are commonly experienced normally by most people during the hypnogogic state, which occurs just prior to sleep.

To Sleep: To Dream

The idea that an altered state of consciousness can facilitate the retrieval of anomalous information is not new. Modern researchers have noted that optimal effects may be linked to certain attentional states. Meditation, dreaming, hypnosis, mental imagery, and sensory deprivation are some of the ways that have fostered the ability to have OBEs, and to do remote viewing.

Anecdotal accounts of apparent paranormal phenomena recur frequently in the early literature of hypnosis and meditation. Similarly, in traditional meditation texts, psi effects or siddhis were claimed to be natural by-products of a state of abstraction in which there is a diminution of ego-boundaries and self-object differentiation. Many disciplines teach that meditation encourages psi but that these are irrelevant side-effects and distract from meditation's major goals.

Sleep is the most common altered state of consciousness and dreaming the most frequently reported mediator of spontaneous paranormal responses. Dream studies, in which sleeping subjects were able to retrieve information sent to them during the night by a "sender," were conducted at the Maimonides Medical Center Sleep Laboratory in the 1970s.

Historically, ascetics, shamans, hermits, and other god-seeking individuals sought out solitude and there are reports of these individuals experiencing what we now call OBEs. Isolation tanks and other means of perceptual isolation have superseded the hermit's cell, and OBE experiences continue to be reported.

Charles Honorton introduced the Ganzfeld procedure to parapsychology research and it quickly became popular. The Ganzfeld combined solitude with sensory reduction, and mental and physical relaxation, and quickly showed itself to be a strong psi-conducive method. There were criticisms of the methodology by Hyman but these were countered and the research continued to give significant results.

However, there has been little research comparing altered states of consciousness and remote viewing, in its many varieties. It may be that an altered state is not needed. For example, the PEAR Laboratory at Princeton University has a huge, significant database of remote perception trials, performed by ordinary people under many different circumstances. There is an old saying that "the proof of the pudding is in the eating." It is possible that different approaches to remote perception, using various states of consciousness, might work for many individuals, rather than one state or one particular method.

References

Baruss, I. 1986-1987. "Met analysis of definitions of consciousness." *Imagination, Cognition and Personality.* 6: 321–329.

Braud, W.G., and L.W. Braud, 1975. "The psi conducive syndrome," 17–20. In J.D. Morris, W.G. Roll and R.L. Morris. Eds. *Research in Parapsychology* 1974. Metuchen, New Jersey: Scarecrow Press.

Castaneda, C. 1968. *The teachings of Don Juan - A Yaqui way of knowledge.* New York: Ballantine.

Child, I.L. 1985. "Psychology and anomalous observations: The question of ESP in dreams." *American Psychologist.* 40: 1219–1230.

Duval, S. and R.A. Wicklund. 1972. *A theory of objective self-awareness.* New York: Academic Press.

Glickson, J. 1986. "Psi and altered states of consciousness: The missing link." *Journal of Parapsychology.* 50: 213–233.

Honorton, C. 1974. "State of awareness factors in psi activation." *Journal of the American Society for Psychical Research.* 68: 243–256.

James, W. 1904. "Does consciousness exist?" *Journal of Philosophy, Psychology and Scientific Method.* I: 477–491.

Jaynes, J. 1976. *The origin of consciousness in the break-down of the bicameral mind.* Boston: Houghton Mifflin Company.

LeDoux, J.E., D.H. Wilson, and M.S. Gazzaniga. 1977. "A divided mind: Observation on the conscious properties of the separated hemispheres." *Annals of Neurology.* 2: 417–421.

Mead, G.H. 1934. *Mind, self and society.* Chicago: University of Chicago Press.

Natsoulas, T. 1978. "Consciousness." *American Psychologist.* 33: 906–914.

Natsoulas, T. 1983. Addendum to "Consciousness." *American Psychologist.* 38: 121–122.

Ornstein, R. 1977. *The psychology of consciousness,* 2nd ed. New York: Harcourt Brace Jovanovich.

Stanford, R.G., and B. Mayer. 1974. "Relaxation as a psi-conducive state: A replication and exploration of parameters." *Journal of the American Society for Psychical Research.* 68: 182–191.

Ullman, M., Krippner, S., and A. Vaughan. 1973. *Dream telepathy*. New York: Macmillan.

Wasson, R.W., and V.P. Wasson. 1957. *Mushrooms, Siberia and history*. Vol.II. New York: Pantheon.

Whitman, J. *The psychic power of plants*.

Woodburn, H. 1975. "The pathology of boredom." *Scientific American*. (Jan. 1975).

APPENDIX B

HISTORY

Historical Considerations

The belief in astral or soul travel has remained an intercultural belief for centuries. Dean Sheils took data for sixty different cultures from anthropological research files and found that fifty-four of them made some mention of an OBE state. Forty-five percent of these claimed that most people could attain an OBE state and could travel outside the body under certain conditions. Another forty-three percent claimed that only a few select people could achieve an OBE. The remainder of the cultures sampled merely mentioned that the belief existed within their particular culture. Sheils concluded that across various cultures some form of belief in OBEs was very common.

Customs and traditions vary greatly between cultures. However, it seems that within these differences there is one particular ability which, although labeled differently, appears to be the same thing—an ability to have OBEs and to access information from remote geographic locations, using something other than the known five senses.

Throughout human history records have been kept of unexplained events which could be attributed to OBEs. In early writings, particularly from the Egyptians, Tibetans, and Greeks, we learn about the belief that the soul was able to fly and existed as a double of the physical body.

The experience of seeing one's double has been called autoscopy or autoscopic hallucinations by the scientific community. However, the phenomenon has been known throughout history and across many cultures. During an OBE the self that is separate from the physical body seems to contain all of the individual's personality, consciousness, will, and even logical thoughts.

From these early spiritual teachings evolved the doctrines of various occult groups such as the Rosicrucians, the Golden Dawn, the Theosophists, and the Kabalists. Some of the leading figures of the early Cabalistic groups called the Rose-Cross (Rosicrucians), which was founded in 1888, were Eliphas Levi and the Marquis Stanislas de Guaita who "loosened the girders of the soul" through magical and alchemical works.

Theosophical Teachings on Astral Travel

In Theosophical teachings an OBE is interpreted as a projection of the astral (or spirit) body from the physical. Madame Blavatsky, in 1875, founded the Theosophical Society in New York where she, and later Bessant and Leadbeater, studied Eastern religious teachings and incorporated them into Theosophical doctrine. According to Theosophist thought, people are not just the product of the physical body but a complex creation consisting of multiple bodies, each one more subtle than the one preceding it. There are thought to be seven great planes of existence with seven corresponding or complementary bodies. One of these, the astral body, is thought to be able to travel on the astral plane, connected to the physical body by a silver cord. At death the cord breaks and the astral body is freed from the physical plane.

During all of my travels I have never perceived a silver cord but I may have experienced the seven spirit bodies.

In 1983, when I was vacationing in the Pocono Mountains of Pennsylvania I liked to swim in a small lake called Deer Trail Lake. When I could not get to Pennsylvania I traveled mentally to the lake and swam in the cool water. During one of these OBEs the swimming "I" split into seven selves, that followed each other to shore, swimming one behind the other. As the selves reached the shore they reintegrated into one "I."

David-Neal Manifests a Tulpa

Theosophical thought also encompasses the concept of "thought forms," the idea that all physical objects, including ourselves, have exact copies or duplicates in the astral realm. Anecdotal evidence for this concept may have been evidenced by Madam Alexandra David-Neal, a French-woman who studied extensively with Tibetan lamas during the early part of this century. During her rigorous training she endeavored to manifest a thought-form or tulpa.

Madam David-Neal visualized her tulpa as "a monk, short and fat, of an innocent and jolly type." However, he became so real to David-Neal that she began to see him in three-dimensional form. Eventually, others saw him too and he became almost malevolent in his behavior. David-Neal had to force him to return to wherever he had originated.

The Blue Nun of Agreda

From the 17th century we have records of a Christian nun, Sister Mary, who became known as the "Blue Nun of Agreda." Between 1620 and 1631 she was, apparently, able to travel in an OBE from her convent in Spain to Central America. There she preached and taught the Jumano Indians. Nobody saw her leave the convent and her superiors labeled her confessions of her travels as "hysterical tales." However, her story was corroborated. Father Alonso de Benairdes was given the official task of converting the Indians and was mystified to find that someone had been there before him. In a letter to the Pope and Phillip IV of Spain in 1622 he told how a mysterious "lady in blue" had visited the Indians before him. She had distributed crosses, rosaries, and a chalice, with which they celebrated Mass.

When Father Alonso returned to Spain in 1630 he heard about Sister Mary's extraordinary claims. He was able to question her in detail and discovered that she was able to tell him many things about the Indians that could only come from living with them. She knew details of the Indians' folklore, their customs, and about their villages.

Father Alonzo received signed statements from Sister Mary's superiors to verify that she had not left the convent, and was astonished when the church elders recognized the chalice, which the Indians has been using, as having come from their own convent. It was estimated that the "Blue Nun" had made over five thousand visits to the Indians and that she had visited different tribes living thousands of miles apart.

The Bilocation Case of Alphonsus Liguori

A famous case of verified bilocation (or of being seen in two places at the same time) comes to us from the eleventh century. On September 21, 1774, a monk named Alphonsus Liguori was at his monastery in Arienze, Italy. While he was preparing for Mass, putting on his vestments, he fell into a deep sleep. He stayed in the coma for two days and when he awoke he claimed that he had just returned from the Pope's bedside in Rome and that the Pope had just died. In those days Arienze was four days journey from

Rome; it was also before the age of modern communications.

Liguori's colleagues attributed his claims to have been a dream. Eventually, news of the Pope's death reached them. They learned that attendants at the Pope's bedside had seen and talked to Liguori, and he had led them in prayers for the dying Pope.

The Notorious Count St. Germain

One of the most mystifying men who has ever lived was the Count St. Germain. The Count began making his fabulous claims in eighteenth century Europe where he was dismissed as an eccentric. Horace Walpole and Voltaire both wrote about the Count. Voltaire described St. Germain as the man "who never dies and knows everything." Count St. Germain claimed that he had discovered the Elixir of Life and the Philosopher's Stone, that he could enlarge diamonds, make gold from lead, and silk from flax. It is claimed that three of his students were the occultists St. Martin, Mesmer, and Cagliostro. Count St. Germain described experiences similar to OBEs, "for quite a long time I rolled through space. I saw globes revolve around me and earths gravitate at my feet."

It seems incredible that with such historical and ethnic documentation of a phenomenon so extraordinary, that so little is recognized by twentieth-century science.

Consciousness-Matter Interactions

Lyall Watson, in *Gifts of Unknown Things*, offers some interesting insights into the factor we call consciousness. He claims that consciousness is experience. It is an unmeasurable something associated with the brain but which is not the brain. Watson likens the relationship of consciousness with matter as light to matter. Matter can influence the motion of light and, he feels, that somehow the same process is implicated when considering matter and consciousness. Maybe there is a reciprocal interaction between matter and consciousness. Body and mind may be able to separate and affect each other in subtle ways. Alex Tanous, an adept out-of-body experiencer, once said that the "Out-of-body experience combined intuition, insight and total body experience in the act of really observing."

Francis Hitching suggests that OBEs may be responsible for other historical feats and phenomena, such as the abilities of Tibetan lamas to traverse great distances.

Waking Dreams

Having established that OBEs exist across time and cultures, just what are OBEs and how and when do they occur? Alan Landsburg writes that projections of any length are nearly always part of the dream sequence. I cannot agree with him on this. Mental travel is just as likely to occur during waking as sleeping states, if the right conditions are present. Having said that, I agree that it is possible for OBEs to occur during sleep, perhaps to be revealed as lucid dreams.

Charles Tart Studies Robert Monroe and Miss Z.

Possibly some of the earliest experimental research in the investigation of OBEs has been carried out at The Mind Science Foundation by Charles Honorton, at the Maimonides Medical Center via the remote viewing experiments of Russell Targ, and at Stanford Research Institute by Harold Puthoff.

During Dr. Russell Tart's research physiological measures were taken and certain correlates were noticed during the time that Robert Monroe had an OBE. Tart found that a drop in Monroe's blood pressure occurred during an OBE; there was also an increase in eye movements, increased alpha and a predominant theta brain-wave pattern, which was typical of meditative states. Tart's conclusion was that these results indicated that Monroe was fluctuating between sleep stages One and Two, and that his OBEs were a mixture of dream-state and possibly ESP, despite the fact that Monroe felt that his OBEs were very different from his dreams.

Robert Monroe developed the Monroe Institute which now offers seminar programs and audio learning systems on cassette tapes and CDs. They enable others to explore expanded states of awareness through various exercises and techniques, using what they call the Hemi-Sync© process. The Hemi-Sync© process involves the use of autohypnosis, relaxation and breathing techniques, enhanced placebo effect, imagery, and specifically sequenced stereo sound patterns called binaural beats that can assist in creating appropriate brain-wave states. Some people have OBEs as an integral part of their experience while participating in the Hemi-Sync© process.

The Demographics of OBEs

John Palmer, a psychologist and parapsychologist, and his colleagues initiated a series of experiments and surveys in the mid-1970s, specifically to gain a further understanding of the OBE. The proportions of people who have experienced an OBE varies but it is commonly agreed that about one person in twenty may have had an OBE during their lifetime. Such factors as sex, age, race, birth order, political views, religion, religiosity, education, occupation, and income appear to be totally unconnected to the ability to experience an OBE. However, Palmer and his colleagues did find that there was a significant relationship between having OBEs, past meditative experience, and having other mystical experiences.

Palmer was able to identify one hundred people who had OBEs and nearly sixty percent of them said that they had seen their body from "outside." Fewer than thirty percent reported "traveling" in the OBE state and only five percent of these people had acquired information via ESP while having an OBE. Interestingly, about ten percent of them had appeared as an apparition to someone else.

According to surveys carried out by researchers Green, Poynton, Blackmore, and the Society for Psychical Research in England, between seventy and eighty percent of single-case OBEers had seen their own body during an OBE, and many of them felt that they possessed a second conscious body. However, less than ten percent ever saw the silver cord that is supposed to connect these two bodies: the physical and the spiritual.

The ASPR and Alex Tanous

During the early 1970s, Dr. Carlis Osis had advertized for subjects who could have OBEs to visit the American Society for Psychical Research to be tested. One hundred people answered and took part in experiments. However, most of them, even though they claimed to have been "out of body," got the target wrong.

In 1975, Osis developed a device that presented a target that could only be seen in its entirety from a certain viewpoint. This optical device consisted of a viewing window looking towards four quadrant pictures consisting of black and white outlines, a color wheel, and a series of mirrors. When viewed from a perspective other than through the window, the target could only be seen as fragmented parts. Alex Tanous, a psychic, was tested with this device, and his results approached significance.

Tanous was tested on other occasions by Osis at the ASPR and he was able to initiate voluntary OBEs to locate target rooms where he perceived objects and caused a feather to move. Tanous saw his "astral body" as a ball of light. This ball was small and able to travel to various locations at will. Dr. Osis decided to see if sensitive equipment could detect this light. An experiment was set up at the New York headquarters of the Energy Research Group by Dr. Richard Dobryn. This group was able to utilize extremely sensitive light-detection equipment which was able to pick up and measure bursts of light in the room when Tanous visited it during an OBE. Tanous was also reported to have been seen by a psychic, in a target room at the ASPR, while he was having an OBE.

The ASPR and Ingo Swann

I first came across a reference to artist and researcher Ingo Swann in a report by Landsberg. Swann has been quoted as saying that he does not believe that the ability to experience an OBE is a special talent but a natural function of human consciousness—something that everyone can achieve. Swann claims that he can control his travels to a large degree, that he can select a specific location and go to it. He can also project himself to a destination, which he knows only by latitude and longitude, and with remarkable accuracy can give a detailed description of the place. Among those who have studied Swann are Osis, Mitchell, Puthoff, and Targ.

Though not considering himself "psychic," Swann presented himself as a subject at ASPR in 1971. Swann was tested by Mitchell to see if he could detect hidden targets that were placed on a platform suspended ten feet above the ground. The objects most easily recognized during such tests were those with bright colors and clear-familiar shapes. Glossy pictures and objects made of glass did not work well. Swann is unusual in that he does not fall asleep during his OBEs and is able to verbally report on his perceptions. He is able to control his OBEs to the extent of initiating and terminating them in response to an audible signal.

During the ASPR sessions, Swann's psychophysiology measures were recorded, including his EEG which was found to contain decreased alpha and increased beta brain waves, in contrast to Monroe's. However, Swann's OBEs occurred during the waking state while Monroe's OBEs occurred during light sleep. It had been suggested by various researchers that there may be no distinctive physiological signs that indicate that an OBE is taking place and that it can occur under many different conditions.

Stanford Research Institute (SRI)

In 1972, Swann offered to be tested by Puthoff and Targ at SRI, after reading a paper of theirs invoking quantum physics as a possible explanation for extra-sensory perception. During the earliest testing at SRI, Swann was accurately able to describe the features of a uniquely designed magnetometer buried six feet in concrete beneath the floor. He also affected the output signal of the magnetometer on a strip chart recorder.

Eventually, Puthoff and Targ initiated "Project Scannate," remote viewing by coordinates, which was suggested to them by Swann. Swann and other viewers, including Pat Price, were provided with latitude and longitude, and they attempted to view the geographical location at those coordinates. Swann and Price were remarkably accurate.

Further rigorous testing of Swann, Price, photographer Hella Hamid, and others at SRI convinced Targ and Puthoff that remote viewing was not just an ability to be enjoyed by certain psychics but that almost anybody could do it.

In 1977, Targ and Puthoff published the results of their remote viewing experiments in *Mind-Reach* in which they evaluated the ways in which remote viewing could be put to practical use. They listed: a) Survival value—many spontaneous OBEs occur at the time of a serious accident, injury or during surgery. "It is in primarily life-threatening situations that exceptional spontaneous functioning seems to occur," they say; b) Executive ESP—use of remote viewing and other anomalous abilities in the business world; c) Futuristic predictions; d) Medical diagnosis; and, e) Space exploration.

The possibilities for the peaceful use of OBEs and remote viewing are endless and, as the phenomena becomes more recognized, new uses will undoubtedly be found. To have the ability to travel out of the body and access information not normally perceived by the regular senses, and to not acknowledge the ability, is like having functional ears and eyes and wearing earplugs and a blindfold.

OBEs have been linked to the supernatural and the magical but only in the past hundred years has the mystery been uncovered to find the hidden reality. Monitored by scientific equipment, modern shamans and witches fly away to search for hidden objects, people, and locations. Occult magic has made way for science.

Stuart Harary and the Psychical Research Foundation

In reports published by the Psychical Research Foundation, the foundation's then-director, Robert Morris described the experiences of another subject, Stuart (Blue) Harary. Harary, an ex-undergraduate at Duke University claimed to have OBEs which occurred at night during sleep. Harary claims to have had OBEs since early childhood but for many years did not tell anybody about them for fear that they would think he was crazy. They hold no religious overtones for him, they are simply experiences that he believes many people have, or could have if they knew how.

According to Morris, Harary used the time prior to experiencing a mental trip as a time of relaxation and separation, which included imaging the target destination. Harary said that once he got to a certain state he could not help but have an OBE.

Morris wanted to see if Harary, in his OBE form, could be detected, and so he was asked to visit a succession of animals during his trips. These animals included small rodents, two kittens, and a snake. The rodents showed no behavioral change, but during his trips to see the two kittens it was found that one kitten showed a response to him, but the other did not. He had chosen both kittens from the same litter; the first because it showed an affinity towards him, and the second as company for the first. It was this first kitten that showed the response during the OBE.

When Harary made an OBE trip to the caged snake, it began striking and gnawing, which was said to be uncharacteristic of the snake's general behavior. There was no statistically significant mechanical detection of Harary's OBEs. The measuring devices showed small unexplained changes but these were not sufficiently correlated with the OBEs.

When a spectrum analyzer (used to detect a wide range of electromagnetic radiation) scanned Harary, more positive results were seen. On one occasion, there was a burst of activity which lasted almost exactly the duration of the OBE, and on four other occasions there was an increase in activity during OBEs.

Psychophysiological variables were also measured during Harary's OBEs including respiration, heart rate, and pulse volume, and these changed significantly from the time Harary was preparing for an OBE and when he was actually having the experience. Respiration, heart rate, and pulse volume all increased while eye movements and skin potential decreased significantly. Differences between the brain wave voltages between the right and left sides of the brain were also recorded.

In addition to the investigations carried out by Morris, another researcher, Dr. William Roll, tested Harary's ability to hear music during an OBE. Selections of music were played in a room a quarter of a mile away from the subject. Harary would initiate an OBE, travel to the music room and then identify the music upon his return to his body.

Jack Houck and the Magical 7.8 Hz

Researchers have recently come to understand that there may be specific brain-wave frequencies that appear to enhance the ability to have an OBE. Researcher Jack Houck has asked: What if the ability to do remote viewing, PK, and other high performance mental techniques could be induced with high-tech means? Houck says that there is some evidence that there exists a mental access window or MAW when the predominate frequency of an individual's electro-encephalograph (EEG) measures 7.81 to 7.83 Hz. This is the same frequency range in which slight oscillations in the earth's magnetic field occur, known as the Schumann Resonance.

Houck first learned of this idea from Dr. Bob Beck when he purchased a simple EEG biofeedback unit from Beck. The unit provided auditory feedback of brain activity to the user. Beck suggested that he and Houck make a recording of an input signal of exactly 7.81 Hz. Houck listened to the EEG unit attached to his head in one ear, while simultaneously listening to the 7.81 Hz recording in the other ear.

After a few minutes of relaxing, the two sounds became very similar and then Houck experienced a full-blown OBE. Of the 45 people who have tried the device at this frequency about one-half have reported a full or partial out-of-body experience. Interestingly, Houck found that some people, particularly psychics and geniuses, have strong components of their natural EEG frequency in the MAW range, even in their awake state.

Positive Side Effects of Remote Perception

An interesting positive effect of having an OBE has been expressed by OBEers. Many have claimed that they no longer feared death and their mental health and social relationships had improved since having an OBE. Whatever follows our physical demise is seen to be the next fascinating adventure.

We are entering a new era where many areas of study, once thought to be unfit subjects for research, are now becoming legitimate. I began this research in the spirit of free enquiry and my hope is that it will add to the increasing respectability and eventual acceptance of these phenomena by the scientific community.

References

Blackmore, S.J. 1982. "Have you ever had an OBE? The wording of the question." *Journal of the Society for Psychical Research.* 51, 791: 292–302.

Broad, W.G., and L.W. Broad. 1975. "The psi conducive syndrome." In J.D. Morris, W.G. Roll, and R.L. Morris,

(Eds). *Research in Parapsychology* 1974. Metuchen, New Jersey: Scarecrow Press. 17–20.

Budge, E.A.W. 1967. *Egyptian Book of the Dead*. New York: Dover Publications.

Castaneda, C. 1968. *The teachings of Don Juan - A Yaqui Way of Knowledge*. New York: Ballantine Books.

Coxhead, D. and S. Hiller. 1970. *Dreams - Visions of the Night*. London: Thames and Hudson.

David-Neal, A. 1971. *Magic and Mystery in Tibet*. New York: Dover Publications.

Evans-Wentz, W.Y. 1960. *The Tibetan Book of the Dead*. London: Oxford University Press.

Hitching, F. 1978. *The World Atlas of Mysteries*. London: Book Club Associates.

Holroyd, S. 1976. *Mysteries of the Inner Self*. London: "Great Mysteries Series." Aldus Books.

Honorton, C. 1974. "State of awareness factors in psi activation." *Journal of the American Society for Psychical Research*. 68: 243–256.

Houck, J. 1994. "Mental Access Window." Presented paper at the TREAT VI Conference, Virginia Beach, Virginia. April 27–May 1, 1994.

Kendrick, T.D. 1967. *Mary of Agreda - Life and Legend of a Spanish Nun*. London: Routledge & Kegan-Paul.

King, F. 1975. *Magic - The Western Tradition*. London: Thames and Hudson.

Landsburg, A. 1977. *In Search of Strange Phenomena*. London: Corgi.

Monroe, R.A. 1985. *Far Journeys*. Garden City, New York: Doubleday.

Morris, R.L. 1974. "The use of detectors for out-of-body experiences" (Summary). In W.G. Roll. "Studies of communication during out-of-body experiences." *Journal of the American Society for Psychical Research.* 71, 1:1–21.

Morris, R.L., S.B. Harary, J. Janis, J. Hartwell, and W.G. Roll. 1978. "Studies of communication during out-of-body experiences." *Journal of the American Society for Psychical Research.* 72, 1: 1–21.

Osis, K. 1973. "Towards a methodology for experiments on out-of-body experiences" (Summary). In W.G. Roll, R.L. Morris, and J.D. Morris (Eds). *Research in Parapsychology* 1973. 78–79. Metuchen, New Jersey: Scarecrow Press.

Osis, K. 1975. "Perceptual experiments on out-of-body experiences" (Summary). In J.D. Morris, W.G. Roll, & R.L. Morris (Eds). *Research in Parapsychology* 1974. 53–55. Metuchen, New Jersey: Scarecrow Press.

Osis, K., and J.L. Mitchell. 1977. "Physiological correlates of reported out-of-body experiences." *Journal of the Society for Psychical Research.* 49: 525–536.

Palmer, J., and C. Vassar. 1974. "ESP and out-of-body experiences: An exploratory study." *Journal of the American Society for Psychical Research.* 68: 257–280.

Palmer, J. 1974. "Some new directions for research." In *Research in Parapsychology,* W.G.Roll, R.L. Morris, and J.D. Morris, (Eds). 53–55. Metuchen, New Jersey: Scarecrow Press.

Palmer, J., and R. Lieberman. 1975. "The influence of psychological set on ESP and out-of-body experiences." *Journal of the American Society for Psychical Research.* 69, 3: 193–213.

Palmer, J., and M. Morris. 1975. "A community mail survey of psychic experiences." In *Research in Parapsychology,* J.D. Morris, W.G. Roll, and R.L. Morris, (Eds). 130–133. Metuchen, New Jersey: Scarecrow Press.

Palmer, J. 1976. "ESP and Out-of-Body experiences: A Further Study." In *Research in Parapsychology* 1975.

J.D. Morris, W.G. Roll, and R.L. Morris. 102–106. Metuchen, New Jersey: Scarecrow Press.

Palmer, J. 1979. "A community mail survey of psychic experiences." *Journal of the American Society for Psychical Research.* 73: 221–252.

Puthoff, H.E., and R. Targ. 1976. "A perceptual channel for information transfer over kilometer distances: Historical perspective and recent research." *Proceedings of the IEEE.* 64: 329–354.

Puthoff, H.E., R. Targ, and E.C. May. 1981. "SRI protocols for remote viewing," revised 1981, and "Experimental psi research, implications for physics." In *The Role of Consciousness in the Physical World.* AAAS Selected Publication 57. Boulder, Colorado: Westview.

Sharkey, J. 1979. *Celtic Mysteries - The Ancient Religion.* London: Thames and Hudson.

Sheils, D. 1978. "A cross cultural study of the beliefs in out-of-the-body experiences, waking and sleeping." *Journal of the Society for Psychical Research.* 49, 775, 697, 741.

Targ, R., and H. Puthoff. 1977. *Mind Reach: Scientists Look at Psychic Abilities.* New York: Delacorte Press.

Tanous, A. 1975. "Out-of-the-body experiences." *New Horizons.* 1, 5, 231–232.

Tart, C.T. 1967. "A second psychophysiological study of out-of-the-body experiences in a gifted subject." *International Journal of Parapsychology.* 9, 3: 251–258.

Tart, C.T. 1968. "A psychophysiological study of out-of-the-body experiences in a selected subject." *Journal of the American Society for Psychical Research.* 62, 1: 3–27.

Tart, C.T. 1969. "A further psychophysiological study of out-of-the body experiences in a gifted subject." (Summary). *Proceedings of the Parapsychological Association.* 6: 43–44.

Tart, C.T. 1981. "Transpersonal realities or neurophysical illusions? Towards an empirically testable dualism." In R.S. Valle and R.V. Eckartsberg (Eds). *Metaphors of consciousness*. 216–222. New York: Plenum Press.

Wasson, R.Q., and V.P. Wasson. 1957. *Mushrooms, Siberia and history, Vol. II*. New York: Pantheon.

Watson, L. *The Romeo error*. London: Coronet Books.

AMERICA, RUSSIA, AND REMOTE VIEWING

Russian Parapsychology

Parapsychology or psi is one of the disciplines that studies extraordinary human capabilities including anomalous human energy transfer and information processing. While the history of western parapsychology has been well documented, that of Russia is not so well known. This chapter takes a look at Russian psychology's attitude to the study of parapsychology, OBEs and remote viewing, its history, contemporary trends, and whether an international information gap exists between America and Russia.

In western terms, parapsychology is a field of study involving research on the informational and energetic possibilities of the psychic and biophysical activities of living organisms. Parapsychology investigates the complex of phenomena relating to the interaction of living organisms with each other and with the surrounding environment without the mediation of the known sense organs or of presently identified energy transfer systems. Western parapsychologists refer to this complex of phenomena as extrasensory perception (ESP) or psi.

Say Nyet to Psi

Western and Russian researchers use different terminology to understand the same phenomena: thus parapsychology, psi phenomena and ESP become biocommunication, psychophysiology, psychotronics, psychoenergetics and biophysical effects in Russia, and the Russian terms biocommunication and bioenergetics covers the western areas of telepathy and precognition, and dowsing and psychokinesis, respectively. Some of the criticisms of Russian psi research have focused on the fact that much of the research has been conducted in a laissez-faire manner with little concern for scientific methodology, and that many claims of psychics and healers have been taken at face value.

Bekhterev and Vasiliev: Early Russian Researchers

Russian research in parapsychology began with the early work of V.M. Bekhterev, neurologist and educator, and L.L. Vasiliev, and this early research was conducted, according to Kozulin and Pratt, within established academic situations and along carefully regulated lines. One of the most important pre-Revolutionary developments in Russian psychology was the establishment by Bekhterev of the first experimental psychophysiological laboratories in Kazan in 1885, and in St. Petersburg in 1895. The Psychoneurological Institute was established as a multi-disciplinary institution that included students, scholars, and physicians studying the human subject from all possible perspectives.

It has been questioned whether Bekhterev's pioneering activities in parapsychology contributed to his unpopularity. Bekhterev shared Dubrov's belief that all animals could communicate telepathically and he was the first person to design ESP tests for dogs that eliminated any sensory cues that might pass, consciously or unconsciously, between trainer and animal. Bekhterev became interested in the entire psychic spectrum and set up a special scientific commission to study human telepathy.

Following the death of Bekhterev in 1928, his colleague Vasiliev established a network of European parapsychological centers focusing his research on establishing a physical basis for telepathy, and this work continued until the economic and political upheavals of World War II. Vasiliev regarded his contribution to be a better understanding of the nature of psi rather than independently proving its reality.

Nina Kulagina

Vasiliev is credited with discovering and studying the psychokinetic abilities of Ninel S. Kulagina. Prior to her death in 1991, Kulagina was observed and filmed in demonstrations of her ability to move small objects and her work has recently been documented by Kireyev. Other feats demonstrated by Kulagina were the formation of a personal biofield of 1000 watts, the generation of heat and sonic waves, and the ability to turn ordinary water acidic. However, permission to test her was denied to American and German governments on the grounds that "parapsychology is not studied in the Soviet Union."

In 1963 Vasiliev presented a paper on telepathy at the Second All Russian Congress on Psychoneurology in Petrograd. The Congress recognized the importance of further research and recommended the participation of Russian scientists in the work of the International Committee for Psychical Research.

The Decline of Psi Research in the USSR

In 1968 the USSR Academy of Sciences fully recognized psychology as an independent scientific discipline in which higher degrees could be granted, and in 1971 the Institute of Psychology was instituted within the USSR Academy of Sciences with Lomov as director. However in 1972, despite these advances, when American scientists, including Stanley Krippner, wanted to organize a series of informal meetings on parapsychology in Moscow they were told that the Psychology Society of the USSR could not support the project because parapsychology was not a branch of scientific psychology.

According to Pratt the political turn of events surrounding the transition from the Kruschev to the Brezhnev era made it more difficult for parapsychological research to be done openly within university laboratories. Naumov, and other interested individuals, worked to build up public interest via the popular press and through correspondence and meetings between Soviet and foreign enthusiasts.

In 1973 the Society of Psychologists assessed the status of parapsychology and issued a paper presenting compelling evidence that developments in parapsychology in the USSR had advanced so far that it could not be ignored by established science. Pratt suggested that there are two interpretations to be made of this: that the time had come for parapsychology to be officially recognized and pursued as a legitimate endeavor; and that public and scientific interest had become so strong that only by officially organizing and regulating the topic could it be tolerated and contained. Perhaps both interpretations are correct.

Was There Really a Psi Gap?

One of the myths that has circulated in the parapsychology field has been that the Russians are many years ahead of us in the field of parapsychology research. I suspect that this rumor, that Russia was spending billions on psi research, was started to generate funding in the United

States. Actual funding for parapsychology in America has been abysmal. Small private groups have kept the field afloat but more and more research groups are disappearing.

Visiting Russian parapsychologists, however, tell us that the same state of affairs exists in their country. The major laboratories have closed due to lack of funding and there has been a proliferation of "kitchen table" and basement labs. Equipment is begged or borrowed and frequent solicitations have been received in the States to fund Russian parapsychological research.

The Race for Information

In fact, there has been a race but never an information gap in parapsychological research between the United States and Russia. Russian psi researchers have told some interesting stories about how the state of research in America has been constantly monitored and replicated. For example, following the pioneering work in remote viewing at SRI, a group at Mundelein College in Chicago replicated their research. In designing their experiments, the Chicago group allocated a time period of thirty minutes for subjects to reach and view the geographic target that they would be telepathically sending to a receiver. The Russians replicated the Chicago experiments and discovered that the thirty-minute gap was the optimal time needed to send telepathic messages. They did not realize that this amount of time had been picked arbitrarily.

Official Recognition for Psi Research in Russia

Russians researchers have also told us that a similar state of affairs existed regarding official recognition of psi, as existed here in the States. The majority of the Russian psi research was done under the auspices of the elite USSR

Academy of Sciences. However, when results were presented to the higher governmental authorities they were classified, then ignored. Now that Russia has become more open, it would be extremely interesting for someone to search the USSR Academy of Sciences Archives and to compare Russian and American research. According to Russian psychologists Dubrov and Pushkin, contemporary civilization, with its information explosion, presents humankind with ever-increasing demands, and ordinary human capabilities are no longer sufficient in the face of the expanding rate of change in work and life.

As Russia undergoes chaotic change, scientists there have enjoyed a freer theater for their views and ideas. Some scientists coming to the west, such as Eduard Naumov, Vasily Nalimov, and Andrei Berezin, have given new insight into the mechanisms of Russian science, and its attitude towards psi research. As of the late 80s there seemed to be a renewed interest in researching paranormal phenomena. In *Science in the USSR*, the official journal of the USSR Academy of Sciences, there were no articles pertaining to psi phenomena prior to 1989, when they published two tentative, critical articles on UFO phenomena. Since then the journal has published articles on ESP, Kulagina, the Russian psychic, psychotronics, clairvoyance, and a short history of parapsychology.

Sanctioned by the USSR Academy of Sciences, several scientific institutes have been researching psi phenomena but judging from papers in Science in the USSR and videotapes of their work, they do not seem any further forward than their American counterparts. Furthermore, psi research is not now being conducted by psychologists but by physicists and medical researchers. The terminology that has been adopted, such as psychotronics and bio-information exchange, relates to the current disciplines, such as physics and medicine, that are carrying out the research.

The Institute for the Study of Theoretical Problems

One such research institute, the Institute for the Study of Theoretical Problems (ITP), which was part of the USSR Academy of Sciences, is located in the Arbat section of central Moscow among foreign embassies and behind the Ministry for Foreign Affairs. The four-story edifice was built in the mid-1800s and, at one time, must have been a magnificent building with its wide staircases and large halls. During my visit to ITP in 1991, there was building debris and scaffolding everywhere, and the central court-yard of the building was filled with garbage.

ITP employed about thirty people, mostly theoretical physicists/engineers and operated on a contractual basis to business, government, and the military. ITP maintained some secure areas of the building for military research and although I was not allowed access to these areas I was introduced to some of the researchers.

Topics being studied on a theoretical basis at ITP included: ionic transfer across biological cell membranes, electro-magnetic effects on DNA, and DNA modeling. Andriankin is also involved in the modeling of rocket propulsion systems and has interests in many other areas: he supervises Ph.D.-level research for civilian and military personnel, collaborates with other domestic and foreign, civilian and military groups, and is actively involved in the establishment of the Russian Academy of Natural Sciences—a break-away group from the USSR Academy of Sciences. While I was in Moscow I met some of the main people in this new movement: Vladimir Krementsov, Valentina Nikolaeva, and Rimily Avramenko.

In the past Andriankin has collaborated with psychotronic groups in Czechoslovakia, Italy and Germany, notably the Institute of Psychotronics in Prague, and in Lodi, Italy; and ITP has studied problems in the fields of gravitation, geophysics, mathematical modeling, mechanics and cybernetics and, according to an article on Andriankin by Frolova, these disciplines may help science take a fresh look at the nature of anomalous phenomena. Andriankin adds that there is now an entire association devoted to the study of bioenergetics and anomalous phenomena set up under the auspices of the Union of Scientific and Engineering Societies of the USSR.

The Rainbow Bridge

In 1983 and 1984, physicist and psi researcher, Russell Targ, his daughter Elizabeth, and Keith Harary visited the Soviet Union as guests of the USSR Academy of Sciences. In Moscow they were able to discuss remote viewing research with Russian scientists, visit with psychics and carry out some remote viewing experiments between Moscow and San Francisco. They were particularly privileged to work with Djuna Davitashvili, a famous Russian healer. It was rumored that Brezhnev employed the services of Djuna for her healing abilities.

During the remote viewing experiments, Djuna, who was not particularly trained in this ability, accurately described the location of a hidden experimenter, 10,000 miles away in San Francisco. In addition, her viewing was done precognitively, four hours before the experimenter had actually decided on a geographic target.

Targ added that, from information gathered during their visit, it became apparent that psi research was taken very seriously at the highest levels of the Soviet scientific and engineering establishments.

A New Direction for Russian Parapsychology

In 1989 the Committee on Problems of Energoinformative Exchange in Nature was set up by a member of the USSR

Academy of Sciences, V.V. Kaznachayev. Kaznachayev then became the Director of the Institute of Clinical and Experimental Medicine, and later, with A. Trofimov, directed the Siberian branch of the USSR Academy of Medical Sciences, which has been studying distant influence on biological systems, as well as carrying out research on telepathy and healing.

Godik of the Institute for Radio Engineering and Electronics of the USSR was asked by the Soviet government in 1982 to undertake a study of the potentialities of contactless diagnostics and therapy. The dictate given was to study the biofields of persons with extra-sensory perception. The Institute is normally engaged in studying the reception and identification of weak signals from physical fields such as space, the ocean, and the interior of the earth. In addition they are studying the psychophysiological effects of contactless healing via infrared, doppler, sonic, electrical and magnetic field, and optical radiation measurements.

A dichotomy now exists; psi research is officially sanctioned by the authorities but there is little funding. Due to the current political and social turmoil in the country, all of the above institutions are experiencing great difficulty in obtaining funding for equipment and qualified personnel. The participation of psychologists in parapsychology research is minimal; the scientific work that remains funded is conducted in institutes that are concerned with the physical or medical aspects of the phenomena.

The Future of Russian and American Psi Research

In both the Soviet Union and the West, the investigation of psi has endured continuing skeptical criticism from the mainstream scientific community. Resistance has taken many forms and includes stringent requirements for proof, and an almost total rejection by mainstream scientific journals of articles and research supporting parapsychology.

Some of the specific criticisms aimed at psi research, both in the West and in Soviet science, are that it has failed to produce a replicable demonstration of an effect and that there are no accountable theories. Dubrov and Pushkin in 1980 counter this argument by advocating that psi be examined in light of conventional and already established theories.

Dubrov and Pushkin explain how "new physics" has paved the way for fresh perspectives on psi and that contemporary psychologists no longer face the limited choice between mechanistic and mystical explanations of natural phenomena. They add that there should no longer be any need to exclude parapsychology from inclusion as a suitable topic for scientific study because of its uniqueness. Dubrov and Pushkin concluded that neither the complexity of the phenomena nor the obscurity of their mechanisms can justify rejecting this, or any other, body of facts from the system of scientific knowledge.

Traditionally, both in western and in Russian science there has been a resistance to the acceptance of psi phenomena for several reasons: theoretical and methodological failings, the design and conduct of psi experiments, and analytical and statistical flaws, as well as the elusive nature of psi itself. The acceptance of psi research would cause a complex paradigmatic change involving the redesign of the social environment, of information exchange, and our understanding of being human.

The American Government and Hidden Psi Research

Over the past few decades it has become apparent that the American government has taken an active interest in parapsychological research and it has been speculated that, despite denials to the contrary, both America and Russia have spent millions on psychic research.

A 1983 Government Report, "Research into Psi Phenomenon: Current Status and Trends of Congressional Concern," stated that psi might be useful in military intelligence gathering. The use of the mind as a weapon has been postulated and this new field of psychic warfare has been referred to as psychotronics. Psychotronics encompasses use of the mind to learn the contents of top secret papers; detect weapons, vehicles and personnel; affect weaponry through the manipulation of controlling computers; and even controlling or killing enemy personnel.

From the early days of the Navy-funded studies of ESP by the Rhines at Duke University, the sleep-telepathy experiments at Maimonides Hospital in Brooklyn, New York to more recent research in remote viewing carried out by Stanford Research Institute, Science Application International Corporation, the Rand Corporation, and the Army, the government and military in its many forms have been actively investigating paranormal abilities.

Stanford Research Institute was one of the first government-funded institutions to carry out remote viewing experiments. In 1976, the SRI team of Harold Puthoff and Russell Targ published the results of their research in a peer-reviewed journal under the title "A perceptual channel for information transfer over kilometer distances: Historical perspective and recent research." This paper has become a classic, and the abstract of this paper sums up the state of the art, at that time, in the remote viewing field.

Project Scannate

During the active days of remote viewing research at SRI, an event occurred which has intrigued not only the parapsychological community but those in the UFO field too. In his book *Out There*, Ralph Blumm describes how, in the fall of 1985, the Defense Intelligence Agency's (DIA) Directorate for Management and Operations launched Project Aquarius. Blum describes the site of this event as a lead-lined conference hall on the third floor of the Old Executive Office Building, directly across from the White House, in Washington, DC.

Blumm describes how the room filled with staff from the Office of Science and Technology, there to await a demonstration by two SRI researchers and their remote viewer.

The introduction, given by one of the SRI scientists, indicated that what the audience was about to witness was the "existence of a new perceptual channel through which certain individuals are able to perceive and describe remote data not presented to any known sense." What was different about this demonstration was that the viewer would be working only from geographical coordinates—longitude and latitude information.

The viewer, after receiving the coordinates for a target, would describe what he had perceived, then would sketch what he had seen. Finally, from a locked briefcase chained to the wrist of a Science and Technology staff member (who was attached to the Office of Naval Intelligence in Suitland, Maryland) came a satellite photograph. What the viewer had correctly perceived, via coordinates only, was the Russian dacha of Mikhail Gorbachev. What the audience had witnessed was a demonstration of SRI's project called Scannate (Scanning by Coordinates).

Although Ingo Swann was responsible for introducing the methodology of coordinate remote viewing to SRI, it was both Ingo Swann and Pat Price, working with Targ and Puthoff, who are credited with putting the concept into practical application. In fact, Pat Price gave such a detailed description of a super-secret installation, the "Crystal

Mountain Complex" in Virginia, that the CIA became interested and classified the research.

Project Aquarius

Next, at the OTA meeting came a demonstration of remote scanning of the oceans to detect submarine activity. Several photographs of American and Russian submarines were laid in front of the viewer by the Science and Technology staffer. According to Blumm, the purpose of this demonstration was to demonstrate how Project Scannate could be utilized to facilitate the detection of submarines. The viewer would scan and describe the location, by geographical coordinates, of each submarine's current position. As a control, the array of photographs contained one submarine that had not even been built at that point, another was in dry dock. However, as well as efficiently viewing the submarine targets (46 percent correct), the viewer discovered something else. What he saw hovering in the air above the underwater device, and what he drew, was a UFO.

Six months following this introduction to remote viewing by coordinates, the DIA, along with Naval Intelligence, initiated Project Aquarius. Viewers continued to scan the oceans, and over the next fourteen months were to record a further seventeen sightings of "hovering, unidentified objects" over the ocean's surface, and directly over a submarine. These sightings were greeted with derision from some researchers and taken as evidence that remote viewing was nothing more than waste of money.

A Finger in Every Pie

Despite protests by government representatives that they have no interest in psi research there is documented evidence of government-funded psi research. Dr. Rhea

White lists at least thirty major government-funded projects, since about 1960, which have investigated such phenomenon as Kirlian photography, OBEs, spirit possession, post-death communication, ESP, magic, sleep-mediated psi, precognition, human consciousness technologies, psychokinesis, and spiritual healing.

The funding for these projects ranged between seven thousand five hundred to one hundred and forty-five thousand dollars, but the majority were for unpublished amounts. The various projects were funded by the National Institute of Mental Health, the Army, the Veterans Administration, the Navy, the Air Force, NASA, the National Science Foundation, and the Advanced Research Projects Agency.

Most of this government funded research was carried out at conventional educational and medical institutions such as Drexel University in Kansas; UCLA, Department of Psychology; Duke University; Maimonides Medical Center in New York; UCLA, School of Public Health; Washington University; Stanford University; UCLA, Davis; and the University of South Alabama, Psychology Department. Other research was conducted by groups already committed to government contract work such as the Stanford Research Institute.

These documented facts and figures are, of course, unclassified but there have been rumors of "black project" psi research funded by such agencies as the CIA and NSA. It is also speculated that some major psi research institutions have been funded by government funds which have been "laundered" through respectable industrial or private concerns. Recently, I learned that the Rand Corporation was doing quiet research into remote viewing, and Motorola has recently expressed an interest in psi research.

In 1978 psychologist Charles Tart undertook a project to survey his colleagues in the parapsychology community.

Tart polled the directors of fourteen American parapsychological research centers and, according to Rhea White, all but one replied. One of the questions Tart asked was "if the center had been approached by agents or officials of the government, acting in an official capacity, to gather information on parapsychology research." Of the thirteen who responded to this question, eight said that they had never been approached, one had been approached once, and four had been approached several times.

During the time that I was participating as a subject at the Psychophysical Research Laboratories, I was privy to the information that its director, Charles Honorton, was approached directly by a government agency to conduct classified research. He declined the project because he felt that all psi research results should be open to public scrutiny. However, despite this information, I was also informed by several "insiders" that it was suspected that the bulk of PRL's support was government funding.

The Economics of Parapsychology Research

Should the military and other governmental agencies carry out psi research, and, are they still doing so? It is known that Russia has conducted extensive psychic research and, potentially, could gather knowledge about events that America does not have.

Economy is another factor that should be considered when deciding whether the government should fund psi research. One space probe costs the country billions of dollars, millions of pounds of hardware and fuel, and thousands of man hours, just in order to keep ahead in the space race.

Mind-power is inexpensive, and although is not yet as accurate as a satellite camera, it is less wasteful of resources. The accuracy factor could be overcome by using psychic cells, many psychics who could all be given the same tasks and their perceptions computer-collated and organized into meaningful data. Psi Tech has claimed that by using this methodology they can guarantee an 80 percent success rate.

The military use of psi may be self-limiting by reason of a moral failsafe. For instance, if a psychic knows (by regular or paranormal means) that his or her abilities are being misused, "psychic blindness" might occur. The military use of psi may be limited by another factor—a form of dyslexia. There are parts of the brain that have been found to be more actively implicated with psychic functioning, especially for OBEs. These areas appear to be located in the non-dominant hemisphere of the brain. Usually the non-dominant hemisphere, in most cases, does not process verbal language. A subject could go to a designated location with the object of reading certain documents but would fail because of this factor. This factor might rule out remote viewing for many military purposes.

What benefits would there be from active psi research by the military and government? The military has access to finances and other resources that are not always available to other institutions or organizations; and there would be status—psi research by the military would add validity and credibility to the subject of psi, and status to those who research, practice, or teach psi.

As a result of other military research in the past there have been spin-offs (technological advances) which have benefited medicine, industry, and business. Ultimately, there could be beneficial spin-offs from psi research.

The RVers Come in Out of the Cold War

Retired General Albert Stubblebine, former commander of INSCOM, and Colonel John Alexander, once director of the Army's Materiel Command, have been closely associated with Psi Tech. Alexander co-authored *The Warrior's Edge* in which he confirms the reality of remote viewing and psychokinesis, and that they have worthwhile applications in enhancing human performance.

While in the military, Major Ed Dames and Stubblebine studied remote viewing under the tutelage of Ingo Swann, and Dames had trained other intelligence specialists in Swann's techniques. In 1989, after retiring from the army, Dames founded Psi Tech, which offered to remote view for industry, governments, and organizations. Psi Tech, according to promotional literature distributed by the company, consisted of a team of eight remote viewers, six of whom were still active duty officers with Army intelligence or Army special operations. The team had worked on projects to access information about such topics and events as: the Tunguska Explosion; the Russian Phobos II space craft failure; projected future technologies; advanced deep space propulsion technologies; clandestine Iraqi weapons facilities; a relook at the KAL Flight 007 shoot-down; atmospheric ozone depletion; and the Saint-Exupery crash site.

Dames claims that although there are many good remote viewers with natural abilities, his team is trained to a high degree of military precision and in specific protocols (controlled remote viewing) which do not allow for creativity. While Swann was at SRI, he had developed a remote viewing technique that could be utilized by one viewer. Dames expanded this technique to create a consensual methodology, whereby several remote viewers perceive component parts of a target. Their impressions are then evaluated and pooled, additional information is accessed, and a report is written based on this information pool.

An additional feature of Dame's methodology is that the viewers do not always get to know details of the target because this can lead to "frontloading," whereby known information can influence the viewing leading to access of erroneous material. Instead, the remote viewers are assigned an arbitrary number that Dames has associated with the target. Surprisingly, this works.

Dames viewers are taught to sit alone in a quiet room with a stack of plain paper, to make notes, and to draw what they perceive. The viewers do not analyze what they see. Dames stresses the importance of emotional detachment during the viewing, and suppression of imagination—both factors which could interfere with the integrity of the viewing. According to Psi Tech literature, Dames offers a 100 percent money-back guarantee on information that is reported to his clients and charges between $6,000 and $8,000 per project.

The National Research Council Report

Further evidence that the government still maintains a close interest in psi research came about through the publication in 1987 of a report by the National Research Council (NRC) which evaluated psi research in terms of human potential enhancement techniques that could be of use in the military. The NRC's evaluation of the field was generally negative and critical. These techniques included sleep-learning, neuro-linguistic programming, psi communication with plants, hypnosis and human-machine interaction.

Fault was found by the NRC with the design and conduct of psi experiments including: inadequate precautions against "sensory leakage"; inadequate security provisions; improper randomization provisions; feedback; incomplete documentation; and inconsistency of conditions and procedures.

Additional factors such as analytical and statistical flaws were an issue: multiple testing for "effect size"; underestimation of the effective error rate and over-estimation of the actual significance level; and erroneous use of statistical procedures.

During the OTA (Office of Technology Assessment) workshop which followed the NRC report most of these issues were discussed and defended, and several suggestions were made for strengthening psi research. The OTA meeting generated another list of criteria, both local and global, which would need to be satisfied before "proof" of psi could be achieved.

It is apparent, from the literature, and from personal observation of the field, that both Russian and American governments, and military, have, in the past, studied psi phenomenon, and are continuing to do so. It is hoped that, as time passes, some of this research will become public and the validity attached to the phenomenon, will then enable orthodox scientists to take up the challenge and continue the study of this fascinating field.

References

Alexander, J.B., R. Grollier, and J. Morris. *The warrior's edge*. New York: Avon Books.

Blum, H. 1990. *Out there*. New York: Pocket Star Books.

Child, I.L. 1985. "Psychology and anomalous observations: The question of ESP in dreams?" *American Psychologist*. 40: 1219–1230.

Dubrov, A.P., and V.N. Pushkin. 1980. *Parapsychology and contemporary science*. New York: Plenum. 17–39.

Dunne, B.J., and J.P. Bisaha. 1979. "Precognitive remote viewing in the Chicago area." *Journal of Parapsychology*. 43: 17–30.

Frolova, O. 1991. "Psychotronics: Unraveling the ESP enigma." *Science in the USSR*. 1: 110–126.

Kaznachayev, V.V., and A. Trofimov. 1991. "Personal communication to the PEAR laboratory." Princeton University.

Kireyev, A. 1991. "Chronicles of discovery and errors." *Science in the USSR*. 2: 54–56.

Kireyev, A. 1991. "Ninel Kulagina: Housewife and medium." *Science in the USSR*. 1: 50–51.

Krippner, S. 1980. *Human possibilities*. New York: Anchor Press, Doubleday.

Kozulin, A. 1984. *Psychology in Utopia: Towards a social history of Soviet psychology*. Cambridge, Massachusetts: MIT Press.

Lapina, M. 1990. "ESP: Can everyone join in?" *Science in the USSR*. 5: 56–64.

Maire, L.F., and J.D. LaMothe. 1975. "Soviet and Czechoslov parapsychological research." United States Army Medical Intelligence and Information Agency (Unclassified). Office of the Surgeon General. 1–71.

McRae, R. 1984. "Psychic warriors: In mind wars." New York: St. Martin's Press. Extract published in *Omni* Magazine, May, 1984.

National Research Council. 1987. "Enhancing human potential: Issues, theories and techniques." (Report of the Committee on Techniques for the Enhancement of Human Performance, Commission on Behavioral and Social Sciences and Education.) Washington, D.C.: National Academy Press.

Ostrander, S., and L. Schroeder. 1970. *Psychic discoveries behind the iron curtain*. New York: Bantam Books.

Personal communication with Dr. Andrei Berezin, biophysicist.

Pratt, J.G. 1977. "Soviet research in parapsychology." In B.B. Wolman (Ed.) *Handbook of parapsychology*. New York: Von Nostrand Reinhold. 883–903.

Psi Tech, Inc. promotional materials.

Puthoff, H.E., and R. Targ. 1976. "A perceptual channel for information transfer over kilometer distances: Historical perspective and recent research." Proceedings of the IEEE. 64: 329–354.

Shaw, A. 1989. "Report on a workshop on experimental parapsychology." Office of Technology Assessment, United States Congress. Washington, D.C.

Staff, 1984. "Psychic war and the Pentagon: Science at the fringe." *Science Digest.* 92, 5: 38.

Targ, R., E. Targ, and K. Harary. 1984. "Moscow-San Francisco remote viewing experiment." *Psi Research.* 3, 3/4: (September/December). 74–82.

Tipikin, E. 1991. "Clairvoyance or catharsis?" *Science in the USSR.* 2: 50–53.22.

White, R. 1989. *Parapsychology: New sources of information.* 1973–1989. Metuchen, New Jersey: The Scarecrow Press.

THE CIA STORY

Nightline Drops a Bombshell for the CIA

The date was November 28th, 1995. Word had been buzzing around the parapsychology community that representatives of the CIA would be appearing on ABC's *Nightline* program with Ted Koppel to discuss their 20 year involvement in remote viewing research. A lot of us hoped that this program would be the long-awaited confirmation and validation of the phenomenon toward which the field had been working so hard.

The time-line leading up to the *Nightline* story began with an earlier program on remote viewing in November by Fox TV's *Encounters*, which had solicited information from the CIA, asking about their sponsorship of remote viewing and other parapsychological research. The agency had sent a letter to *Encounters* (which was shown on the show) stating that not only did the CIA acknowledge that they sponsored research into remote viewing in the '70s but that they, at the request of Congress, were now analyzing remote viewing to see how useful it might be for future intelligence collection.

What actually happened, on the November *Nightline* program, was that ex-Director of the CIA, Robert Gates, downplayed the role of the CIA to that of "monitor" of the remote viewing field; that they, along with other intelligence agencies had only contributed 20 million dollars over 20 years (this amount is peanuts in terms of the amount of money that Federal Budget for Department of Defense research—actual figures for 1995 were 35,350 million dollars), and that remote viewing had not turned out to be the reliable tool they had expected it to be. Gates also denied that remote viewing had been utilized in sensitive intelligence gathering missions.

The Stargate Project

The program centered around a study, carried out by the American Institute for Research, a private Washington social science research firm (commissioned by the CIA at the request of the Senate Appropriations Committee) named Stargate. The motive behind the study was to find out whether more government research into parapsychology was warranted. The study, dated September 29, 1995 was made public by the CIA, supposedly after it was cited by ABC News. The ABC News leak reported that the CIA and "other United States intelligence outfits" had hired remote viewers to spy on political and military targets including the 52 American hostages that had been held for 444 days in Iran after the take-over of the Embassy in November 1979. ABC also reported that remote viewers had been hired by United States spy agencies to pinpoint downed American and Soviet aircraft, as well as to communicate with submerged submarines.

Stargate, authored by statistician Professor Jessica Utts at the University of California at Davis, and Professor Ray Hyman, a psychologist at the University of Oregon at Eugene, found that "statistically significant results had been observed in laboratory experiments to test remote viewing." Utts is reported as saying that the data she had reviewed for the CIA study had produced the "most credible evidence to date that humans were capable of paranormal psychic feats." However, according to *Science News*, December 9, 1995, the two researchers differed sharply over how to interpret the findings.

Representatives for the CIA (Robert Gates, Dale Graff and "Norm"—technical advisor for CIA) interviewed on the *Tonight Show*, told a different story. The CIA and the academic authors of Stargate, on the air, stated that remote viewing had not been shown to be useful for intelligence gathering. Hyman argued that "the occurrence of statistical effects does not warrant the conclusion that psychic functioning has been demonstrated."

An interesting on-line article by Daniel Brandt (March 1996) mentions that "Another of Ted Koppel's CIA guests, identified only as 'Norm' did mention the 'eight-martini' results from some of the experiments."

A spokesman for the CIA, David Christiansan has been recently quoted as saying that "no further United States research into remote viewing was warranted." Christiansan added, "We think the intelligence community shouldn't pursue research on this and that it is best left to the private sector." According to Christiansan, the CIA had carried out research into remote viewing from the early 1970s but had determined it to be unpromising and dropped the idea. The CIA program codenamed Stargate was originally initiated in response to government concerns about a possible "psychic gap" between Russia and America. In 1972, the DIA published a report detailing this supposed gap in psi research between the two countries. It was proposed that the Soviets were undertaking psi research that would enable them to know the contents of top secret United States documents, the movements of American troops and ships, and the location and nature of military installations. They claimed that they might be able to mold the thoughts of key American military and civilian leaders from a distance; maybe even cause the instant death of any United States official at a distance; and disable American military equipment at a distance, including spacecraft.

Stargate Based on Selective Data

The parapsychology community, including those professionals most involved in remote viewing research, were astounded. Questions were asked. Why did the CIA choose to talk about their involvement in remote viewing research now? Who leaked the original story to ABC, and why? Why was the agency downplaying the significance of the RV studies? They thought it strange that the CIA "deep-throat," called Norm on *Nightline*, said that only a dozen of the 500 projects were significant to the agency. Those in the know felt that RV successes had improved over the years and that the current success rate was much higher. Some contributors to the post-mortem suggested that perhaps what was seen on *Nightline* was part of a disinformation campaign "designed to throw the public off the scent of more extensive research being done on technology-enhanced psychic intelligence."

The Stargate Time-Line

The *Nightline* revelations produced a flurry of media attention. An interesting feature article by Jack Anderson and Michael Binstein revealed further information about Stargate. When Anderson and Binstein first reported on the Pentagon's use of psychics back in 1984, the project was called Grill Flame. Later, the project's name was changed to Center Lane, and then to SunStreak. The original project had begun at Fort Meade, also the home of the National Security Agency, and was based on CIA-funded research at Stanford Research Institute. The project's most avid supporters have been Senators Clairborne Pell, Robert Byrd, and Daniel Inouye, and Representative Charles Rose of North Carolina.

According to Anderson and Binstein, remote viewers were employed in the location of a downed Soviet Tu-95 "Backfire" bomber, which the CIA knew had crashed in Africa. There is further corroboration of this particular viewing. According to Col. John Alexander (in an interview for Fox TV's *Encounters* program, November 11, 1995), "There is a case that was reported with the downing of a Soviet aircraft in South Africa. And there was a race between us and the Soviet Union to get to that craft. But neither side was exactly sure where it went down. Using remote viewing techniques, we were able to steer our recovery committee to within 100 meters. And we, in fact, beat the Soviets to the plane." Alexander, while still in the military, worked with the Intelligence and Security Command, where a small unit of viewers operated.

The Three-Letter Agencies and Remote Viewing

Other speculation that the CIA utilized RV information comes from an article by Douglas Waller in *Time* magazine dated December 11, 1995. Waller wrote that the Defense Intelligence Agency "credited psychics with creating accurate pictures of Soviet submarine construction hidden from United States spy satellites"; and a 1993 Pentagon representative said psychics had correctly drawn twenty tunnels being built in North Korea near the demilitarized zone. It was also rumored that one set of Pentagon planners consulted psychics to pinpoint where Colonel Muammar Gaddafi was staying before United States warplanes attacked Libya in 1986.

It has also been reported by Anderson and Binstein that remote viewers had been employed in most international crises over the past two decades. The two reporters stated that during the Gulf War, knowledgeable sources told an associate that remote viewers fingered the secret location of Iraq's Saddam Hussein, though this was never verified by conventional means.

According to Ingo Swann, the key players in project Stargate and the documentation supporting the real story remain under the strictest security restraints. Swann also states that the 15 percent success rate quoted by the CIA on *Nightline* represents results from an early series of viewing at SRI done by a group of beginners and non-trained personnel. The 65 percent accuracy demanded by the military was close to being achieved when the program was dropped in 1995.

Jessica Utts, the Davis professor, stated in *Time* Magazine "Sometimes it seems that these people were right on but nobody knows when those times come."

Joseph McMoneagle

On November 30, a third program put on by ABC called *Put it to the Test* featured Joe McMoneagle, who completed a very successful live remote viewing session. McMoneagle was one of the original military remote viewers at the Fort Meade unit.

In December, some of the periodical media picked up the story. *Time* magazine published a story entitled "The Vision Thing" with the subtitle "Ten years and $20 million later, the Pentagon discovers that psychics are unreliable spies." Douglas Waller outlined the story and concluded that "the three full-time psychics still operating on a $500,000-a-year budget out of Fort Meade, MD will soon close up shop."

"Why All the Fuss?" asks Swann

Someone who has been with the RV program since its inception is Ingo Swann. His view is that nothing that the media is reporting in this latest "flap" is new news. "Media coverage was quite extensive during the 1970s decade regarding this issue," reports Swann. Jack Anderson's syndicated columns covered reports of media involvement in psychic research and other media across the country picked up the lead and republished the stories. Swann faults the media for not checking their archives on this topic while presenting the story as news.

Swann's main contention is that the current reports have one main difference to these earlier reports—this regards the spin being given to today's "media frenzy" over the Stargate report. Reporting of the topic in the 1970s was more matter of fact.

Covert Research Still in Place?

There are some writers, particularly Joe McMoneagle in his book *Mind Trek*, who assert that the covert government programs, after being denounced by the CIA, have now gone back underground. That is possible. There are plenty of Black projects where such a program could be hidden. It seems highly unlikely that such a successful program would be scrapped in its entirety. The government is wasteful but it is not stupid. Perhaps, one day we will hear the rest of the story.

APPENDIX E

THE CRITICS

Is an OBE an External or Internal Event?

One of the major questions asked in the OBE research literature has been whether some aspect of human consciousness actually leaves the body, or whether we are traveling within some internally generated imaginal world, or whether we are tapping into some vast source of information, similar to the ancient concept of the Akashic Record.

There seem to be four major schools of theory regarding OBEs and these are:

- That a physical double travels in the physical world;
- That a physical double travels in an astral world;
- That an astral double travels in the astral world; and,
- That an astral double travels in the physical world.

From my own experience I favor the first of these interpretations. Practical evidence of this autonomous state was evident during a recent commissioned remote-viewing where I was given only the coordinates of my destination by a third party. At the target destination, while I was viewing the location, I felt as if waves were washing over my body. This gave me the idea that perhaps I had triggered some warning device or sensor at the target.

After submitting my report, I received feedback on the target. In fact, I had sensed underground alarms that were present at the target. These were radio-controlled and sensed movement and vibration. This site was easy to view from an aerial location but the nearer I got to the ground, and the nearer to the sensors, the more difficult it became to view it. This remote viewing give me an indication that some physical part of consciousness had been at the site.

According to critic and parapsychologist Susan Blackmore, "An OBE is an experience in which a person seems to perceive the world from a location outside their physical body. In this state they can see and hear events and conversations that cannot be perceived from their actual physical location."

However, whether anything actually leaves the body during an OBE is a debatable point. Proponents of the occult view of OBEs see astral travel in an astral world as self-sustaining evidence that the soul can leave the body at will and leaves permanently after death. Grosso argues that there is always part of our consciousness that is separate but we only become aware of this fact during an OBE.

Parapsychologist Robert Morris writes that an OBE may be the evidence we need that indicates that the self is capable of leaving the body, temporarily, during an OBE, then permanently at death. The concept that "something" is able to temporarily be separate from the physical body is supported by ASPR researchers Osis and Mitchell.

This pro view is countered by the advocates of psychological theories that state that nothing leaves the body, that the astral body and the astral world are nothing but the products of imagination, and that OBEs cannot be put forward as evidence for survival after death. Osis criticizes these theorists as reducing the OBE experience to "nothing but a psychopathological oddity."

Other advocates of the psychological theory have suggested that the OBE is nothing more than a reliving of the birth experience, that it is basically an act of narcissism, and a denial of our inevitable mortality.

The Parapsychologist/Critic Symbiotic Relationship

Blackmore has suggested that an OBE begins when a person loses contact with sensory input from the body while remaining conscious. She proposes that the person retains the feeling of having a body, but that feeling is no longer derived from data provided by the senses. The experiencer views the world from perceptions that arise in the brain rather than from direct sensory input. Blackmore sees a major dilemma with the concept that something actually leaves the body during an OBE. If the body that is "out" is non-physical in nature, she cannot see how it can interact with the physical environment. If, on the other hand, it is physical, we should see more evidence of its presence. She claims that the evidence of paranormal functioning during OBEs is very limited and unconvincing.

The OBE, Blackmore adds, may best be viewed as just another altered state of consciousness (ASC) and that everything perceived during the OBE is the product of a combination of memory and imagination. She suggests that during an OBE the imagination may be more vivid than in the individual's waking state. The following are necessary, she says, for OBEs to occur:

- Vivid and detailed imagery;
- memories and images that may seem real;
- reduced bodily sensory input;
- maintenance of awareness and logical thinking.

However, Blackmore's theories do not explain cases where the individual, during an OBE, has been seen at a distant location by a witness, or when the OBEer is able to access verifiable information regarding a distant location or event.

Parapsychologist John Palmer also doubts the idea that something leaves the body during an OBE. He says, "The experience of being out of the body is not equivalent to the fact of being out." He also disputes the concept that psychic phenomena can occur during an OBE which he views as a private experience which may or may not turn out to be one associated with ESP. Basically, his view of OBEs is that they are very personal experiences akin to imagination.

However, Palmer has very definite ideas of what happens during an OBE. He suggests that the experience almost always occurs during a hypnogogic state, that visual state just before sleep, when input from the senses are at a minimum. During the hypnogogic state the individual's sense of identity becomes threatened and the mind attempts to establish a sense of normality by creating an inner imaginal world. To avoid this apparent threat, perceptual changes take place within this virtual world, giving the impression that some part of the individual is separate from the physical body. This state of affairs might be psi-conducive only in that it encourages internal attitudes and expectations known to facilitate psychic phenomena.

Stephen LaBerge supports Palmer's and Blackmore's idea that the OBE is caused by the loss of external sensation. This OBE state, he suggests, may occur just at the onset of sleep, while the individual retains consciousness but is passing from waking into REM sleep. The conscious mind then creates an efficient simulation of the outside world within which an OBE can occur. LaBerge feels that the dream and OBE worlds that we create reflect the potential vastness that exists within the human mind and that these internal worlds feel as real as our waking world.

Once again, this explanation does not explain how the person having the OBE is able to access verifiable information from the outside world.

Just What is Extrasensory Perception?

J.B. Rhine, of the early Duke University parapsychology laboratory, now the Institute for Parapsychology, had defined ESP to cover "any instance of the apparent acquisition of knowledge without the use of the known senses." This includes clairvoyance, where the individual could acquire knowledge about physical objects or locations, and precognition, knowledge related to happenings prior to their actual occurrence.

Over the past thirty years, many scientific groups have tried to evaluate remote viewing, trying to understand the phenomena. However, because of the controversial nature of the experience it has come under strong attack from various critical groups on the grounds that it is not an appropriate topic for scientific investigation. In fact, psi has been criticized for belonging to a class of topics collectively called pseudo, or false, science.

According to Paul Kurtz of the Committee for the Scientific Investigation of Claims of the Paranormal (CSICOP): ". . . not all of the claimants to scientific knowledge are able to withstand critical scrutiny and many turn out to be pseudo, or false, sciences."

If this is the case, what distinguishes a scientific research method from a pseudoscientific one? What is pseudoscience, who defines its current usage, and does the term pseudoscience have validity in the scientific search for knowledge, particularly that regarding remote viewing?

CSICOP (or PsiCops as some of the parapsychological community call them) is a skeptics' organization which claims to encourage the critical investigation of paranormal and fringe-science claims (pseudoscience) from a responsible, scientific point of view. It also attempts to disseminate factual information about the results of such inquiries to the scientific community and the public.

However, the group does not appear to carry out any objective scientific inquiry, even though their membership contains many "blue-ribbon" elite from major American universities.

CSICOP's publication *The Skeptical Inquirer* contains interviews and articles written purportedly from an objective, skeptical viewpoint, but which frequently degenerate into bickering, name-calling, and debunking. Highly prestigious scholars are affiliated with CSICOP and its subsidiary organizations, as well as a number of magicians. One of these magicians, James Randi, was successful in creating a hoax at one of the early parapsychological laboratories that forced it to close and discontinue research.

Project Alpha

Skeptic Jim Lippard relates what happened to the McDonnell Laboratory in St. Louis, Missouri, when Randi executed "Project Alpha." "Project Alpha was a hoax devised by Randi to test parapsychologists. He had two teenage magicians, Steve Shaw and Mike Edwards, pose as psychics and they arranged to be tested at the McDonnell Laboratory, which had just opened as a parapsychology laboratory in St. Louis. Shaw and Edwards were believed to be genuine psychics and a presentation about them was given at the Parapsychological Association (at which most parapsychologists were not taken in). Randi himself suggested controls to the laboratory, which were imposed on Shaw and Edwards, and they ceased to produce results.

The McDonnell Laboratory published nothing about these two men, but two other psi researchers, Berthold Schwartz and Walter Uphoff, did. Randi then revealed the hoax publicly (which indicated that the two young men used radio-communications to relay information between them and fool the researchers who thought they were communicating psychically). Randi exposed the fraud and awarded the laboratory director, Peter Phillips, the "straight spoon" award.

Subsequently, parapsychology laboratories have installed "fail-safes," and other procedures to prevent such an event happening again, and most invite skeptics and magicians to advise on experimental procedures. If a magician can create the same effect as the psychic, further experimental controls are needed.

The Magician/Parapsychologist Symbiosis

One such skeptic and magician, Daryl Bem, a psychologist at Cornell University, was invited to evaluate the Ganzfeld research work at the Psychophysical Research Laboratories. The lab utilized the Ganzfeld technique in its research. The Ganzfeld or "whole field" creates a setting of mild sensory deprivation which allows the subject to move into the inner world of the mind. This is achieved by isolating the subject, seated in a comfortable chair, in a darkened room, listening to "white noise" through earphones. Halved ping-pong balls taped over the subject's eyes are flooded with red light to create a homogenous visual field.

During the Ganzfeld, Honorton and his colleagues had subjects, or "participants" as PRL preferred to call them, try to "perceive" or view a video target that was being played in another isolated room, and being watched by a "sender." The "perceiver" would talk out loud during the session, commenting on the visual images that flashed through his mind, and then would rate either four still pictures or four moving videos, to judge which one he felt the "sender" was watching during the session. The process was completely automated, which excluded a lot of the judging problems encountered in the early days of psi research.

Bem admits that he was initially skeptical of the claims, made by Honorton and others, that the Ganzfeld was psi conducive. However, through participating in the research and installing appropriate experimental controls, Bem and Honorton were able to report statistically significant results. Bem and Honorton published their findings in a peer-reviewed journal, the *Psychological Bulletin*, a first for such controversial results. Sadly, Honorton, who was completing studies at the University of Edinburgh in Scotland, died in 1992, before the paper was published.

Honorton's research has been subjected to ongoing criticism from the scientific and skeptical community. During the mid-1980s psychologist and skeptic Ray Hyman and Honorton were embroiled in a lengthy paper debate regarding the Ganzfeld work. Bem and Honorton's recent paper has also come under attack but the skeptics agree that the statistics are impressive and that the results defy explanation within the conventional paradigm. Bem remains convinced of the results and hopes that their findings prompt others to replicate the effects. Hyman has suggested that all these results should then be pooled into one large study, a met-analysis, which may reveal further information about the phenomenon.

Science or Pseudoscience?

Parapsychology has been called a false science or pseudoscience by many scientists. Kurtz, one of parapsychology's foremost critics, states that "the term 'pseudoscience' has been used in many ways but that one must be careful not to apply it indiscriminately." He feels that the term should be used for those subjects that clearly meet the following criteria: that do not utilize rigorous experimental methods in their inquiries; lack a coherent, testable, conceptual framework; and/or assert that they have achieved positive results, though their tests are highly questionable, and their generalizations have not been corroborated by impartial observers. While this definition sounds reasonable, accusations of pseudoscience have been voiced in other contexts such as in Radner and Radner where the emotive use of the term is positively rabid.

These marks of pseudoscience are characterized by the Radners as: the absence of credentials, anachronistic thinking, looking for anomalies, the use of myth, a grab-bag approach to evidence, production of irrefutable hypotheses, arguing from spurious similarity, explanation by scenario, research by exegesis, and refusal to revise in the light of criticism. They add that having just one of the marks is a sufficient condition for being labeled pseudoscience.

Criticisms of the critics have been voiced by the Rockwells to the effect that "while the rationalists need not be infallible in their fact and judgement, they need to remain open-minded and argue rationally." The Rockwells accuse the critics of using false categorization, personal defamation, group derogation, unsubstantiated allegations, contradictions, nonsequiturs, rumor and innuendo, appeals to authority, and apocalyptic rhetoric in their denouncement of pseudoscience.

Siever warns about the use of words that can be used judgmentally in characterizing the differences among the sciences. Terms such as "hard" and "soft" science could be interpreted as "good" or "bad" science, just as pseudoscience can be used indiscriminately. Accusations of pseudoscience have been thrown at such widely varying topics as: parapsychology, fundamentalist creationism, astrology, numerology, cryptozoology, UFO research, and palmistry.

The critical community has been accused of using the term "pseudoscience" for a variety of self-serving ends such as censorship, and as elitist militancy. These have no place in the free pursuit of knowledge. "Pseudoscience" is not a valid term when it is used indiscriminately, loosely, or as a political or social tool for a minority group. Polkinghorne points out that the property of humanness is always undergoing historical change and development and can never be fully defined. Therefore, the methods of investigating human experience cannot be defined within the narrow confines that the critics propose.

Parapsychology 101

I hope that scientific research into OBEs and remote viewing will continue, expanding our knowledge and understanding of the phenomena. While the critics are extreme in their definition of what constitutes reasonable topics for scientific research, their criticisms serve a useful purpose in guiding future research along lines that would provide useful critic-proof knowledge.

Why has there traditionally been such a resistance to the acceptance of psi phenomena such as OBEs and remote viewing? The modern field of study known as parapsychology emerged directly from 19th-century "psychical research," which investigated phenomena such as telepathy and clairvoyance, as well as having its early roots way back in human cultural history. The field became established in 1882 with the organization of the Society for Psychical Research (SPR), in England, whose goal was organized scholarly research. The American counterpart to the SPR, the American Society for Psychical Research (ASPR) was founded in New York in 1885.

The Greek letter "psi" has been used to denote the study of the social sciences and psychology but has a specialized usage in defining the scientific study of paranormal phenomena such as precognition, clairvoyance, and telepathy (collectively termed extrasensory perception or ESP) and psychokinesis (PK). John Beloff of the Psychology Department at Edinburgh University adds that the term psi, as the generic expression covering both ESP and PK, has become part of a new vocabulary for parapsychology.

Robert Jahn of Princeton University's Engineering Anomalies Research Laboratory has described the various major categories and subcategories of psi as:

1. **Extrasensory Perception (ESP)**
   a. Telepathy
   b. Clairvoyance
   c. Precognition/Retrocognition
   d. Animal ESP

2. **Psychokinesis (PK)**
   a. Physical Systems
   b. Biological Systems

3. **Survival**
   a. Reincarnation
   b. Apparitions
   c. Mediumship

4. **Out-of-Body Experiences (OBEs)**

Precognition is best described as foreknowledge of an event or condition prior to its occurrence. Precognition has been described by Gertrude Schmeidler, both as the process underlying the acquisition of prior knowledge and to designate psi information about the future. Precognition can occur in the waking state or in dreams, as in precognitive dreams about a future event.

Clairvoyance can be described as the extrasensory acquisition of information about an object or event, involving only one single individual and the event occurring in real-time, (as opposed to precognitive), whereas telepathy may be interpreted as "mind-to-mind" communication, where the perceived information occurs in another person's subjective experience.

Psychokinesis or PK is the apparent ability to influence physical objects or events by thought processes.

Some researchers, such as Jahn, suggest that the field of psi can be thought of in terms of a process of information and/or energy exchange which involves inanimate consciousness in a manner not currently explicable in terms of human science. Attempts have been made to link psi with the processes of quantum mechanics, a new concept in physics.

Resistance to the Acceptance of Psi

The investigation of psi has endured continuing skeptical criticism from both the mainstream scientific community and from special interest groups, such as CSICOP. Resistance by the established scientific community has taken many forms, including the stringent requirements for proof imposed on psi research, an almost total rejection by mainstream scientific journals of articles and research supporting parapsychology, and the public, derisive form of criticism practiced by some members of CSICOP.

Some of the more commonly cited concerns regarding psi research have included:

- demonstrable fraud;
- naivete of technique, including inadequate controls, faulty equipment, sensory cuing of participants, selective treatment of data, improper statistical methods and general theoretical and experimental incompetence;

- little improvement in comprehension over years;
- absence of adequate theoretical models;
- suppression of negative results;
- poor experimental replicability;
- elusiveness of effects under close scrutiny;
- sensitivity to participants, attitudes, and laboratory ambience;
- marginally significant results;
- inconsistency with "scientific" world view.

(OTA Report: 1988)

Some of the specific criticisms aimed at psi research are that it has failed to produce a replicable demonstration of an effect and that there are no theories to account for psi. While these criticisms are arguable, Glickson suggested that recognized models, such as those found in cognitive psychology for instance, could be used to investigate anomalous phenomena.

"It is apparent that psi research needs to be viewed as an interdisciplinary problem," says Robert Morris of Edinburgh University in Scotland. Another general strategy is to look for unresolved problem areas of uncertainty in other disciplines. New branches of science in the past have been able to demonstrate their worth by helping solve problems in existing bodies of knowledge. Alcock stressed that psi research should do more to incorporate its concepts into the theories and models of other areas of inquiry. For example, recent advances in neuroscience and physics could provide explanatory models for psi.

The NRC Report Again

The most recent episode in the continuing controversy over the scientific study of psi appeared in a report by the National Research Council which evaluated psi research in terms of human potential enhancement. The NRC's evaluation of the field was generally negative and critical.

Fault was found by the NRC with the design and conduct of psi experiments including:

- inadequate precautions against "sensory leakage";
- inadequate security provisions;
- improper randomization provisions;
- feedback;
- incomplete documentation;
- inconsistency of conditions and procedures.

Additional factors such as analytical and statistical flaws were an issue:

- multiple testing for "effect size";
- underestimation of the effective error rate and overestimation of the actual significance level;
- Erroneous use of statistical procedures.

During the OTA workshop which followed the NRC Report most of these issues were discussed and defended, and several suggestions made for strengthening psi research:

- employment of impeccable experimental equipment and technique, using highest possible precision;
- separate marginal effects from background noise;
- concentrate on statistical replicability;
- utilize "tripolar" protocols;
- maintain equal respect for the aesthetic/impressionistic and rigorous/analytical aspects of the research.

The OTA meeting generated another list of criteria, both local and global, which would need to be satisfied before "proof" of psi could be achieved. Local criteria had to do with statistical significance and power, with experimental methodology and controls. Also, it was noted that the current "skeptics" constantly alter their concept of proof.

Global criteria would present an overall pattern that the scientific community would be forced to recognize and accept. These criteria would include replicability, lawfulness, consistency of effects, and cumulativeness across time.

Is Psi Research Following the Rules?

Is there any suggestion that psi research is already following these rules? According to some psi researchers such as Charles Honorton, Gertrude Schmeidler, Roger Nelson, and Dean Radin, it appears that at least in two areas, in replicability and lawfulness, these criteria are being followed. The following illustrates how psi research is working in one area towards achieving criteria that would contribute to the acceptance of psi within both the scientific and skeptical communities.

Schmeidler has addressed one of the major criticisms directed at psi research: that parapsychology does not have a theory. She maintains that "a theory of psi has been held for over a hundred years: the theory that psi is a psychological process." In order to evaluate the theory that psi is a psychological process she reviewed the psi research which relates to psychological findings such as: the experimenter effect, group psychology, personality traits, mood, altered states of consciousness, perception, learning and memory, and other brain/body factors. It is possible, she concluded that psi is processed in the same manner as ordinary perception.

According to Hansel, a critic and researcher from Swansea, Wales, the acceptance of psi research would have to lead to a renewal of our concepts of how we interact with our environment:

Parapsychologists claim that some people have the ability to perform such acts as identifying objects when the conditions normally assumed to be necessary for their execution are absent. Such behavior, they call extrasensory perception, or ESP. If people can act in this way new processes have to be admitted as underlying brain activity and the manner in which organisms interact with the environment. The existence of ESP would thus be of profound significance not only to the understanding of human behavior but also to science in general. It would signify that there are processes in nature so far undiscovered that permit ESP to exist.

The Potential Benefits and Harms of Psi

Robert Jahn has looked at the potential benefits of psi; the acquisition of fundamental knowledge, practical applications, and humanistic benefits: "New mechanisms for transfer of information or energy might be identified or broader understanding of those properties and how they are perceived and measured might emerge."

Recently an outraged Princeton University physicist, Philip Anderson, gave, perhaps, a precognitive view of the chaos that would be caused in the hard scientific world if psi were accepted:

If such results are correct, we might as well turn the National Institute of Standards and Technology into a casino and our physics classes into seances, and give back all those Nobel Prizes, since the measuring apparatus with which we think we have been achieving all this precision can actually be bent out of shape by the first Uri Geller who comes along, and our vaulted precision is all in our heads.

There has been a resistance to the acceptance of psi phenomena for several reasons: theoretical and methodological failings, the design and conduct of psi experiments and analytical and statistical flaws, as well as the elusive nature of psi itself. The acceptance of psi research would cause a complex paradigmatic change involving the re-design of our social environment, of information exchange and our understanding of being human.

The Hard Sciences Venture into Psi Research

There is much speculation about what would happen if the hard sciences, such as physics, decided to enter the parapsychological arena. This is already happening. In Russia, researchers from other disciplines, such as physics and medicine, are venturing into the psi arena. In Canada, Dr. Stanley Jeffers, a physicist at York University has been replicating some of the psi research conducted at Princeton University's PEAR Lab. Nursing schools are researching human-to-human interactive psi processes in the application of therapeutic touch, a process which has been shown to lessen patients' pain and anxiety, and hospitals are setting aside "prayer rooms" where nurses can meditate or pray for their patients. Research has shown that when nursing staff set aside time to do this, it reduces the length of hospital stay and lessens costs.

It is my belief that within the next five to ten years, the hard sciences will become increasingly interested in the field of anomalies. Even the terminology of psi is changing, reflecting the interest that orthodox science is taking in the psi process. The term "human-machine interaction" now reflects PK research on the interaction between humans and electronic devices. Remote sensing, perception and viewing has replaced clairvoyance, and biocommunication is coming into favor to replace telepathy.

Pragmatic Applications of Psi

Practical applications, long thought of as the process through which psi would gain acceptance, are in place. There are at least four groups around the continental United States that are attempting to put remote viewing onto a practical, business basis. These groups solicit private clients, in industry and commerce, and in government, to carry out disciplined technical remote viewing.

My prediction for the discipline of parapsychology is that it will gradually be assimilated by orthodox sciences especially as the New Physics contemplates the role of the observing human mind (consciousness) in the production of physical events. A new terminology will be adopted, such as cyberphysiology (the role of consciousness and self-regulation), and psychotronics (technical applications of psi). In all fairness, let us hope that the valuable contribution made by the parapsychological community is not forgotten but that their persistent research be acknowledged and will form a base for many exciting new future ventures.

References

Anderson, P.W. 1991. "On the nature of physical laws." *Physics Today*. December 9.

Bem, D.J. and C. Honorton. 1992. "Response to Hyman." *Psychological Bulletin*. 115: 25–27.

Blackmore, S.J. 1982. *Beyond the body: An investigation of out-of-body experiences*. London: Heineman.

Glickson, J. 1986. "Psi and altered states of consciousness: The missing link." *Journal of Parapsychology*. 50: 213–233.

Grosso, M. 1981. "Towards an explanation of near-death phenomena." *Journal of the American Society for Psychical Research*. 75: 37–60.

Hansel, C.E.M. 1985. "The search for a demonstration of ESP." In P. Kurt (Ed). *A Skeptic's handbook of parapsychology*. 97–128. Buffalo, New York: Prometheus.

Jahn, R.G. 1982. "The persistent paradox of psychic phenomena: An engineering perspective." Proceedings of the IEEE. 70: 136–170.

Kurtz, P. 1978. "The paranormal: science or pseudoscience?" Outline of a lecture at The Smithsonian Institution, April 19.

Kurtz, P. 1985. "Is parapsychology a science?" In P. Kurtz (Ed). *A skeptic's handbook of parapsychology*. Buffalo, New York: Prometheus.

LaBerge, S., and L. Levitan. 1991. "Other worlds: out-of-body experiences and lucid dreams." *Nightlight Newsletter*.

Morris, R.L. 1974. "The use of detectors for out-of-body experiences." (Summary). In W.G. Roll. "Studies of communication during out-of-body experiences." *Journal of the American Society for Psychical Research*. 72, 1: 1–21.

Morris, R.L. 1987. "Parapsychology at the University of Edinburgh." *University of Edinburgh Graduates Journal*. 45–49.

National Research Council. 1987. "Enhancing human potential: Issues, theories and techniques." Report of the Committee on Techniques for the Enhancement of Human performance, Commission on Behavioral and Social Sciences and Education. Washington, D.C.: National Academy Press.

Osis, K. 1975. "Rival models for ESP." *New Horizons*. 1, 5: 230–231.

Osis, K., and K.L. Mitchell. 1977. "Physiological correlates of reported out-of-body experiences." *Journal of the Society for Psychical Research*. 49: 525–536.

Palmer, J. 1974. "Some new directions for research." In W.G. Roll, R.L. Morris, and J.D. Morris (Eds). Research in Parapsychology. 1973. 53–55. Metuchen, New Jersey: Scarecrow Press.

Palmer, J. 1978. "Consciousness localized in space outside the body." In D.S. Rogo (Ed). *Mind beyond the body: The mystery of ESP projection.* 35–51. New York: Penguin Books.

Palmer, J. 1978. "ESP and out-of-body experiences: An experimental approach." In D.S. Rogo (Ed). *Mind beyond the body: The mystery of ESP projection.* 193–217. New York: Penguin Books.

Radner, D., and M. Radner. 1982. *Science and unreason.* Belmont, California: Wadsworth Publishing Company.

Response from James T. Lippard to the USENET computer news group system responding to a request for information and a bibliography on Project Alpha.

Rockwell, T., R. Rockwell, and W.T. Rockwell. 1978. "Irrational rationalists: A critique of the humanist's crusade against parapsychology." *Journal of the American Society for Psychical Research.* 22: 23–34.

Schmeidler, G.R. 1988. *Parapsychology and psychology: Matches and mismatches.* Jefferson, North Carolina: McFarland.

Shaw, A. 1989. "Report on a workshop on experimental parapsychology." Office of Technology Assessment, United States Congress. Washington, D.C.

Siever, R. 1968. "Science: Observational, experimental, historical." *Scientific American.* 56, 1: 47–71.

APPENDIX F

THE FINAL ANALYSIS

An Integrative Model of Consciousness

Consciousness theories can be divided into two basic schools: monistic and dualist. Monistic views are the domain of orthodox or conservative science which sees mind and matter as basically the same. Dualism views mind (consciousness) and matter (body, brain) as separate and able to exist independently. A model of consciousness that I have constructed, the Integrative Model, proposes that consciousness can be described both as monist and dualist, and that both schools of thought are correct.

The model that I have formulated is based on a triangular configuration. At the bottom of the triangle, taking up perhaps half of the space, is the cognitive unconscious, consisting of our memories, learned behaviors, abilities, and thought patterns. Taking up two-thirds of the remaining space is our cognitive consciousness which contains our conscious thought processes, logic, and decision-making skills. At the very top is our double consciousness, a small triangle of consciousness which is a duplicate or fractal of the larger triangle. Usually, this double consciousness is an integral part of the whole, represented by the larger triangle, but under certain conditions, such as during an OBE, it can detach and act autonomously, and is not constrained by time and distance. Robert Morris and his colleagues describe this as some "tangible aspect of the self that can expand beyond the body."

The Akashic Record, the Matrix, and Zero Point Energy

Some investigators speculate that whatever is doing the viewing may eventually be measurable, as some type of energy. Our current knowledge of remote viewing understands that whatever medium is involved it is not hindered by Faraday cages (which shield against electro-magnetic radiation), it can function across distance and around the curve of the Earth, and it can be accessed through many miles of sea water; and yet the information contained in the viewing retains its signal strength.

Dr. Hal Puthoff, formerly of the SRI team, has indicated that there may be a physical medium for the remote viewing signal. Its route may be carried or enhanced through the presence of zero-point energy. This energy matrix fills our environment, even in a vacuum. It is possible that this medium may be capable of ferrying information across distance.

It Just Might Be True

There is a saying, from the Chinese Book of I-Ching, that a person can tell whether water is warm or cold simply through personal experience. In the same way, goes the saying, a man (or woman) must convince himself about his own experiences, only then are they real. The same can be said about OBEs and their practical application to remote viewing. I have been testing the water and seeking to assure myself of the validity of my experiences.

In 1983 I reviewed my feelings and attitudes towards the OBE phenomenon. Some of the questions that I had asked myself five years earlier were: "How will I feel if I find some proof that OBEs are valid experiences? What if I can actually perceive events other than with the five regular senses?"

Since then, by personal experimentation and participation with professional laboratories and organizations, I have proven to myself that such an ability exists. However, my perceptions are not always "on-target." Sometimes my OBEs are accurate, sometimes they miss, at other times there are perceptions that are near the mark but cannot be classed as hits.

Time as a Factor of Doing

From personal experimentation I have found that distance and personal contact with the subject of the OBE did make a difference to the outcome of some of my earlier OBEs. I noticed that there was a noticeable dropping off of hits which seemed to correlate with an increase in distance. However, this could have been due to the fact that I personally knew the people connected to the nearer locations. Princeton's PEAR Laboratory has not found this effect in their remote perception research. PEAR has found, over thousands of trials, that remote perception can occur irrespective of time or distance. The remote viewing exercises that I have carried out over the past few years have also been successful regardless of time and distance.

According to the Russian mathematician and philosopher, Vasily Nalimov, time appears to be a function of doing and is susceptible to our own personal level of doing. He sees time as being a very subjective phenomenon, related to whatever activity we are engaged in. We have all had the experience of becoming engrossed in a task and time seeming to pass very quickly. Yet, the same time seems to drag when we are bored or waiting for an event to occur. Time, then, appears to be subject to our psychological state. Perhaps in remote viewing time can be manipulated and past, present, and future become only reference points on the information trail.

A Hit and Miss Affair

I was curious about near-misses and misses in remote viewing. What are they and why do they occur? Are they observations of places visited on the way to or coming back from a destination? Are they imaginary artifacts or mislabeling by the brain? I looked at where the misses and near-misses occurred in sequence in each series of OBE perceptions that I was analyzing. I found that they tended to occur either at the beginning or at the end of a sequence, rarely in the middle, which seemed to support the suggestion that they could be related to information picked up prior to and at the end of a remote viewing.

Puthoff and Targ have a theory about why errors occur in reporting the results of OBEs. Their remote-viewing subjects reported OBEs in great detail but they generally contained inaccuracies as well as accurate statements. They also noted that a left-right reversal was often observed. Essentially correct descriptions of "basic elements and patterns" were often coupled with incomplete or erroneous analysis of "function"; for example, a remote-viewing of a tower of girders would be labeled as a water tower instead of a look-out tower.

Puthoff and Targ saw this pattern of inaccuracies throughout their remote viewing research and came to several conclusions. Paranormal functioning involves specialization of parts of the brain which predominate in spatial and other holistic processing. It is the non-verbal part of the brain that does the viewing and it is only interested in spatial characteristics. When the verbal part of the brain relates what the other part has viewed, some distortion of material occurs and errors are made.

In analyzing my own OBEs I feel that these are valid observations. During an OBE I can rarely read anything. I often reverse left and right orientations, and I have learned to be careful not to label, but to spatially describe targets.

A Gentle Form of Schizophrenia?

There are several questions that have bothered me during my study of the OBE ability. These questions concern the mental ability of persons able to have OBEs, the morality attached to such abilities, and the possible misuse of the experiences.

OBEs have been called dreams, delusions, even hallucinations by skeptics who have not read the vast literature available to support the validity of the phenomenon. Researchers have examined the mental-illness interpretation of OBEs, which had often been referred to by mental-health professionals in terms of "depersonalization" and "derealization," and found that these terms could not validly be applied to the OBE phenomenon.

In the state of depersonalization, the individual feels that their immediate environment becomes unreal and they feel cut off from reality. Derealization refers to the state where an individual believes that their own body does not belong to them, they deny that they feel any emotion, and they experience distortions of time and place. The individual may also experience changes in body image and may even experience events from a point several feet ahead of the physical body.

Major differences between these psychiatric terms and OBEs lie in the fact that imagery is often colorless and dull and there is a loss of imagination. Whereas in the OBE state, imagery contains a full range of veridical color and the imagination retains its vitality.

Capgras Syndrome is another psychiatric condition that has been cited as an explanation for the OBE state. In this condition, the individual believes that a close friend or relative has been replaced by or cloned as an exact duplicate. The patient has great difficulty in believing that this imagined double is actually the friend or relative. It is thought that this syndrome arises when a patient has difficulty in accepting negative personal feelings. However, this syndrome has no resemblance to OBEs where the experiencer feels that they are separate from their own physical body.

According to David Black in *Ekstacy: Out of the Body Experiences*, psychiatrists usually dismiss any OBE as being simply "autoscopy" (the projection of a consciousness unable to accept responsibility for a particular act, a narcissistic hallucination that denies the power of death). He adds that some psychiatrists have suggested that the OBE may be the expression of a "gentle schizophrenia." However, the experience of seeing yourself from outside the body is an extremely rare occurrence in schizophrenia. Black, a freelance writer, was initially skeptical of OBE claims but he became intrigued when he kept encountering such accounts and decided to investigate the phenomenon. Black's bibliography may have been the first to list nearly all of the current OBE references up to the mid 1970s.

Dr. Glen Gabbard, a staff psychiatrist, and Stuart Twemlow, psychologist of the Menninger Clinic in Topeka, Kansas, reported a study of a group of 345 people reporting an OBE and found them to be as emotionally healthy as any group of average Americans. They were physically healthy and above average in intelligence and education. With *The Eyes of the Mind*, he documented their attempts to give a description of the psychological aspects of the

OBE and to differentiate the phenomenon from other altered states of consciousness. Gabbard and Twemlow viewed OBEs as occurring within the range of phenomenon ranging from those that could be interpreted as transformative, noetic, and integrative to those that were clearly pathological. Despite these studies, there still remains a social stigma attached to any behavior which is out of the ordinary.

The Use and Misuse of Psychic Ability

Critics of psychics often ask, "Why can't a psychic predict the winner of the Derby, or make a killing on the Stock Exchange, or become a millionaire?" If someone has paranormal abilities what is to stop that person using their paranormal abilities for personal gain or the invasion of another's personal mental space?

I have come to the conclusion that people who have genuine, natural OBE abilities also have a heightened sense of morality and propriety. Joost A.M. Meerloo has described a fascinating phenomena which seems to occur when a sensitive (a person with paranormal abilities) is asked to use their capacity for a purpose other than that related to service to others. In effect they become "psychically blind."

I believe this blindness is a form of psychic defense learned early in childhood. According to Meerloo: "Telepathic sensitivity has to be trained and carefully guarded. Blurting out to all the world everything one sees or feels means only to expose oneself to mistakes and criticisms but to overstep the boundaries of privacy and reserve every individual is entitled to and should maintain."

I have theorized that in the process of developing psychic talent a parallel process is in progress which has the end result of an increase in individual moral attitude.

Once the validity of OBEs becomes established, peaceful uses for the ability could aid medicine, crime detection, industry and business. Applications could be found in many fields. I also predict that the first computer/brain interface will be through a type of remote perception.

There is a science fiction film where doctors enter the bloodstream of a seriously ill person in a miniaturized submarine. Their mission is to cure the illness. The medical uses of OBEs would not only be limited to observation and diagnosis. The days of diagnosis by technology would be over as an adept would be able to enter a patient's system to examine and report on the condition of each organ. This is not such a far-fetched idea. Already psychics have entered the internal workings of plants via OBEs and described the cellular structure making up the plant. Descriptions have been given of the intricate structure and makeup of the cells, as well as accurate descriptions of the cellular structure, even the precise configuration of the DNA molecules. Vogel has suggested that one day the individual will move into his own cells to destroy the ones causing disease or tumors. The beginnings of this new era of medicine can be seen in the advances made in the field of psychoneuroimmunology.

Remote Viewing and the Law

Psychics are already used by law enforcement agencies to locate missing persons and property and to help solve open cases. Arthur Lyons and Marcello Truzzi in *The Blue Sense* document the involvement of psychic phenomena in modern crime detection. The term "Blue Sense" comes from an anecdote attributed to Dr. C. B. Scott Jones, and related by Lyons and Truzzi, where he was in attendance at a meeting where a well-known Canadian psychic was working with a police artist on a composite sketch of a criminal suspect. As the picture took shape, Dr. Jones notes that the artist seemed to anticipate the changes the psychic would request, almost as if the two men had the same image in mind. When Jones commented on the fact, the police artist smiled and said, "That's what we call the blue sense.' Good cops have it." The "blue sense" named after the common color of police uniforms, is that hunch that sends a cop back to a police station or down an alley; that feeling of impending danger that tells him to draw his gun. It is that unknown quantity in the policeman's decision-making process that goes beyond what he can see and hear and smell.

The book evolved as the first public report of information gathered by the Center for Scientific Anomalies Research (CSAR) under its Psychic Sleuths Project. This program, initiated in 1980, has become an international clearing house for data on police use of psychics, and it now has data on over two hundred psychics who have worked with police and law-enforcement agencies.

For the past five years, many of the ex-military remote viewers have been using remote viewing for humanitarian purposes. Lyn Buchanan's group, Problems Solutions Innovations, applies remote viewing to finding missing people. The Inner Vision Institute has also implemented remote viewing to search for missing children and adults. Other groups are training law enforcement and security organizations to remote view. There is the potential for misuse of remote viewing but, in general, remote viewing has been applied in an altruistic way.

The Future of Remote Viewing

As described in an earlier chapter, in future years remote viewing may be used to locate astronauts lost in space, to seek out lost or nonfunctioning satellites and report on space emergencies. They could work alongside engineers, computer personnel, and medics to add a new dimension to emergency location work.

The mind is able to go where a machine or a physical body cannot go. An adept viewer could enter a hostile environment, encountering flood, fire, chemicals, or other substances. A remote viewer could go out into space, into the hub of a nuclear reactor after a melt-down; the possibilities are endless.

Such a resource would be invaluable to industry. These psi-engineers would be trained in the regular fields to enable them to report and describe potentially dangerous or threatening conditions. They would be non-risk trouble-shooters and their potential would be unlimited.

Several groups have already attempted to utilize remote viewing in the business world by predicting stock market trends or silver prices. As the computer age continues to develop I foresee a more meaningful way for remote viewers to become involved in the world of business. Professor Eyo-Ita writes of his experiences in his homeland of Nigeria which helped formulate his theory of the B3 aspect of consciousness—that aspect that can travel and access information. Eyo-Ita speculates how B3 may enable an individual A to travel in the "astral" to a business meeting while A is delayed at home. At the meeting the B3 of the delayed individual can, he says, stimulate the B3 of several of the other meeting participants B, C, and D, who are then able to share information about the meeting with the remote perceiver, as well as relaying information from person A to persons E, F, and G, who are also present at the meeting.

Applications in the Arts

As computers become more complex and viewers more skilled at interfacing with computers there may come a time when an individual will be able to enter the complex electrical circuitry of a computer, not only to trouble-shoot, but also to interact with the computer. Information that now takes a programmer hours to punch into a computer would perhaps take seconds with a brain/computer link-up.

There are now many software programs which can produce computer music. Computers are becoming so sophisticated that the right combinations of keys will produce a full orchestra of authentic sounding instruments. The state of-the-art in computer technology is taking us to the point where computers can simulate whole orchestras. I envisage a time when individuals will be able to interact with computers to produce music, not by tapping keys, but my manipulating electrical circuits within the computer through psi. Musically gifted psychics would be able to compose, store, and print their creations whilst relaxing in a chair, perhaps even miles away from the computer.

Giving "Sight" to the Blind and "Legs" to the Lame

It might be interesting to explore the possibility that visually impaired people might benefit from being trained in the technique of remote viewing. Visual acuity is probably our most valued sense, next to hearing. We can lose touch, taste, and smell, yet still function reasonably well in daily life. The sense of vision enables us to locate ourselves in relation to other people and objects in our environment and to react accordingly. According to the professional groups who are utilizing remote viewing on a practical basis, the skill can be learned by anybody. Consequently, visually impaired persons should not be excluded from the opportunity of acquiring a new cognitive skill that could perhaps tap into cortical areas, bypassing the damaged visual cortex, and supplement the knowledge they gain about their environment.

Another group that might possibly be helped are the those restricted in their physical mobility, perhaps confined to bed or a wheelchair. Training in remote perception could add another dimension to their enjoyment of life. Modern technology offers the physically impaired many innovative devices to make life easier, but nothing would be as freeing as being able to move out-of-the body into a mental space where there was no handicap. In an OBE the physically handicapped could turn cartwheels, the blind and deaf might see and hear. These are exciting suggestions that I hope some future investigator will follow-up.

Where Do We Go From Here?

Ingo Swann writes:

For remote viewing to have a more positive influence on our future, it must be found useful at the grass roots level where goal oriented individuals can perceive its applications for the common good. Only those individuals who have made some effort to understand it as a personal experience will be in a position to comprehend more fully the potential of it. They are the advanced thinkers who will redefine the boundaries of consciousness.

A commissioned remote viewing, for Intuition Services, following the CIA disclosures in 1996, inquired about the future of remote viewing and how study of the topic could be enhanced. My feelings were that while the main research groups are going to be changing their focus (and funding), they will be going into some exciting new areas. The questions and answers were as follows and are reproduced here with the group's permission:

1. Are there United States government personnel using any type of remote viewing as an intelligence or investigative tool? Describe the scope of the program.

In-house only and very reserved and cautious; program deals with hard facts—no intuitive or right-brain stuff. Directive reads "get away from spoon-bending and all that junk." Perhaps this is a continuation of old research, now in-house but kept under wraps. However, individuals are the same as before and find it difficult to keep their own metaphysical and spiritual values separate from their RV work. The RV work centers around financial matters and the investigation of people and groups.

2. What foreign governments are applying RV in a substantial way? What is driving their use?

Rogue scientists within the Chinese system are attempting to investigate RV in an effort to confront and challenge the current system of values and standards. Although they realize it is difficult to change the system they feel that the RV process gives them an edge in terms of finances and knowledge.

3. Is there a localized receptor in the brain? Is it being used to help monitor ESP performance?

Going against all the known thought on RV, I perceived that both of the cerebral hemispheres play a prominent role in RV. The RV process may be the same as for ordinary perception except that RV is finer-tuned. There is no special ESP receptor. However, the corpus callosum—the bridge of fibers between the hemispheres—plays a role in filtering perceptions.

4. Describe the next major public success story about the application of remote viewing?

After a year or so of media ridicule, a famous NY or DC investigative reporter will take the wraps off of the government cover-up of RV and bring the whole story out into the open. He or she takes up a challenge from a retired member of one of the intelligence agencies to do this story and does a wonderful job. Although the government continues to deny involvement (even when their own people are coming forward), the public begins to take notice. In particular, a few courageous academicians will decide to incorporate RV investigations into several neuroscience studies.

The present climate of skepticism is lifting and the millenium is rapidly approaching, with its promise of radical changes in attitude and perspective. The future is exciting and challenging. Are we ready?

References

Black, D. 1975. *Ekstacy: Out-of-the-body experiences.* 175. Indianapolis: Bobbs-Merrill.

Dunne, B.J., Y.H. Dobyns, and S.J. Intner. 1989. "Precognitive remote perception III: Complete binary data base with analytical refinements." Technical note PEAR 89002. Princeton University Engineering Anomalies Research, Princeton University, School of Engineering/Applied Science.

Eyo-Ita, P. 1993. *Personal experience and the sciences.* (Private publisher-unknown).

Gabbard, G.O., and S.W. Twemlow. 1984. *With the eyes of the mind: An empirical analysis of out-of-body states.* New York: Praeger.

Lyons, A., and M. Truzzi. 1991. *The blue sense.* New York: The Mysterious Press.

Meerloo, J.A.M. 1972. "Sympathy and telepathy: A mode for psychodynamic research in parapsychology." In R. Van Over (Ed). *Psychology and extrasensory perception.* New York: New American Library.

Morris, R.L., S.B. Harary, J. Janis, J. Hartwell, and W.G. Roll. 1978. "Studies of communication during out-of-body experiences." *Journal of the American Society for Psychical Research.* 72, 1: 1–21.

Nalimov, V.V. 1982. *Realms of the unconscious: The enchanted frontier.* University Park, Pennsylvania: ISI Press.

Puthoff, H.E., and R. Targ. 1976. "A perceptual channel for information transfer over kilometer distances: Historical perspective and recent research." Proceedings of the IEEE. 64, 3: 329–354.

Swann, I. 1975. *To kiss earth goodbye.* New York: Hawthorne.

ABOUT THE AUTHOR

Angela Thompson Smith, M.S., is a research psychologist, writer, and lecturer currently living in Las Vegas, Nevada. She was born in Bristol, England and holds degrees in psychology from the University of Wales in Cardiff and Manchester University, England. She is married to David A. Smith, a computer engineer, and has three stepsons—David, Daniel, and Johnathan.

Her professional training and research experience has been in the fields of nursing and social work, parapsychology, consciousness, and cognitive science. Smith has a long and sound background in research and teaching. She has logged in seventeen years of private research, seven years of work in established laboratories (including Princeton University), five years of remote viewing (RV) consulting, and two years of teaching remote viewing. Smith acknowledges that everybody has some RV ability and that remote viewing is a normal, trainable skill. Past RV consulting with Psi Tech, the Intuition Network, and Intuition Services has covered projects ranging from stolen artwork, the Unabomber case, archaeological sites, missing persons, historical enigmas, space exploration, Earth changes, and future technologies.

Smith is a member of the New York Academy of Sciences and the Society for Scientific Exploration. She has appeared on international, national, and local television and radio shows and has given talks to scientific and general audiences. Authorities in the RV field, such as Paul Smith and Lyn Buchanan, have encouraged her work, and Ingo Swann has written the foreword to this book.

Tesla - p. 95

Hampton Roads Publishing Company

. . . for the evolving spirit

Hampton Roads Publishing Company
publishes books on a variety of subjects including
metaphysics, health, complementary medicine,
visionary fiction, and other related topics.

For a copy of our latest catalog,
call toll-free, 800-766-8009,
or send your name and address to:

Hampton Roads Publishing Company
134 Burgess Lane
Charlottesville, VA 22902
e-mail: hrpc@hrpub.com
www.hrpub.com